MW01297103

Do They Care?

The one question all brands should ask themselves, continually.

DOUGLAS SPENCER

v1.2

DEDICATION

To those in this world
who are able to question us all
and, most importantly, themselves.

CONTENTS

Chapter 1: One Question 3

Chapter 2: Do Employees Care?...22

Chapter 3: Do Customers Care?...38

Chapter 4: Why Care About Mergers and Acquisitions?...................50

Chapter 5: Who Else Cares? 66

Chapter 6: Do You Care to Change?...77

Chapter 7: Do You Care? 91

About The Author...101

End Notes..102

ACKNOWLEDGMENTS

My gratitude, first and foremost, to those I call family who have patiently listened to me talk about writing a book for what seems like a decade.

Taylor Wilkins and Michael Minihan for their help with research and writing.

My editor, Susan Reiter.

All the people from whom I learned everything shared in this book. You know who you are.

And to you, yes you, for caring enough about what you do to consider the ideas that follow.

CHAPTER 1: ONE QUESTION

To connect genuinely with anyone, not only do we have to care about them, they also have to care about us. What is true for individuals and families in their interpersonal relationships is also true for companies and their brands, their employees, and their customers.

Think about your daily life:

- Why do some teenagers work half-heartedly?
- Why do some people fail to vote?
- Why do some friends and family put so little effort into giving gifts?

They simply don't care.

The teenager doesn't care because he's totally wrapped up in his own stuff—getting more likes on Instagram, finding the courage to ask a girl out, buying that latest iPhone—you name it. Those priorities are far more important than taking out the garbage, so he just doesn't care.

One vote out of millions cannot possibly have any impact on the outcome of a general election, right? That's certainly a widely held belief. No matter how often they're reminded of the value of their input, many individuals don't believe their vote matters—so they just don't care.

Commercialism has twisted our appreciation of almost all holidays, bastardizing them beyond recognition, obscuring their original significance and emotional meaning. In many families, love is measured in dollar signs, not in tender words, hearty hugs or kind deeds. (As a member of the broader marketing community, I admit that we are more than just a little culpable for abetting this reality.)

When the "what" is more important than the "for whom," we care less about selecting a gift that is unique and valued and more about simply checking off a box. We feel lost and helpless when it comes to gift giving, so we just don't care.

One ingredient makes the difference: caring. Simple conceptually, caring becomes more elusive as we become more distracted, more divided and more distrustful.

Therein lies the problem—as well as the opportunity. When a culture of cynicism affects almost all commercial relationships, smart companies have an opportunity to set themselves apart simply by asking, continually, one simple question: Do they care? Do they care about what you're doing with your products or services? Do they care about how you do it? Do they care about what it does for them? Do they care whether it comes from you or someone else?

Oh, by the way, who is "they"?

"They," in a word, is everyone. "They" is your management team, your employees—the insiders. "They" is your customers, your vendors, even your competitors—the outsiders. Most importantly, "they" is you. In this book we will explore what caring means for all three. We will explore ways brands can earn the care they need to thrive.

In fact, when I first had the idea for this book, my working title was "Make Them Care." It had an impressive ring to it, I thought. Very action-oriented. Very empowering. I could practically hear it screaming from a book jacket.

Then, I realized that making someone care would never work. It's like the iconic Bonnie Raitt lyric: "I can't make you love me, if you don't." You have to earn someone's love. And you have to earn any care your spouse or friends show for you. So by continually asking the question "do they care?" it puts the responsibility on the brand manager to earn the caring from all corners of the community that all strong brands need.

The Cadillac of Caring

My father was born in 1922. The Great Depression hit his family very hard. He often would tell us stories of picking elderberries with his brother only to have his mother make a pie out of them that would serve as the entirety of their dinner. He never ate elderberries as an adult.

As a young boy of ten, he saw his first Cadillac. "It was beautiful," he'd say. "Black, shiny, and big." The man driving it looked successful: well-dressed, confident, a boss. No doubt his family had more than elderberry pie for dinner. "From that moment on," he said, "I was hooked."

That Cadillac served as the beacon he would follow to motivate him until he reached the financial independence he never had during childhood. Every deal, every transaction, every decision had, just below its surface, the image of a new Cadillac.

Finally, in 1975, he bought home a brand new, red Cadillac Coupe de Ville, complete with red leather seats and a white vinyl roof. It was beautiful. It was enormous. It was the happiest day of his life.

In the years just before and during my college education, he downgraded to an Oldsmobile. Perhaps not a drastic change, but a painful one for him, I'm sure. Once my tuition was paid off, however, he went back to driving a Cadillac until the day he died. Even my grandfather, who only went as far as the tenth grade, bought home a new Cadillac each year from 1966 until1984.

My mother outlived my father by 24 years. For the first ten following his death, she continued to purchase a new Cadillac, then moved down to a Buick, admitting to her concern: "What will people think? A woman my age driving a Cadillac?"

"Probably that you like Cadillacs," my sister and I tried to reassure her. Nonetheless, she bought the Buick but never quite warmed to it. At the age of 90, the idea of a new Cadillac was mentioned once again. And within six months there was another new Cadillac, a CTS, in her garage. The engine was still cooling when, after having driven it to church and back, she died of a heart attack in her kitchen at the age of 94.

"Your mother loved that car," one of her friends told me at the funeral. "I think she would have slept in it if she could have." I think so, too.

My mother cared about that brand and what it said about her life. It reminded her of her husband and his focused ambition for creating the stability he never had as a child. My father, in turn, cared about the brand because—and I truly believe this—it gave him hope when there seemed to be none. And it gave him reassurances along the way—a yardstick by which to measure his progress.

They both cared deeply about that brand, even when the financial situation wasn't what it had been. And they always returned, whenever they had to stray for money reasons. You only do that if you care.

Cadillac isn't the only automobile brand that connects with customers at that level. Almost all of today's major car manufacturers have legions of fans who care deeply about their brand of choice.

What does "caring" mean in terms of brand preference? In this context, it means engagement, an openness, and a certain level of internalization. It doesn't mean faking a smile with a customer steps up to the counter. It doesn't mean sending out notes from the CEO to all employees lauding them as "family." And it certainly doesn't mean buying one brand for a while and then switching to the next shiny object that comes along to compete for attention.

Caring is an emotional investment. Caring means that it's not just your analytical side making decisions about the relationship; it means that positive feelings are also data points to consider when a customer makes any decision involving your product or service.

Whether you're an employee, an employer, or a customer, caring is crucial if a strong brand is to emerge and thrive. Let's take a look at how and why.

The Science Behind Caring

Where does caring begin to take root? Why did my father fall so head-over-heels for that Cadillac so long before his career allowed him to buy one for himself?

Well, let's work backward. The word *care* takes its roots from old English and German words *caru, chara* and *carian*, meaning grief and lament. Even its old Norse root means sickbed. Think carrion as in carrion crow, where the word is defined as "the decaying flesh of a dead animal." Though desultory, these melancholy definitions and origins make sense with regard to the human understanding of caring. A natural characteristic of the human condition is the compulsion to care, via empathy or sympathy, for those who are sick, dying or otherwise facing adversity.

We humans tend to most profoundly realize their care for someone or something after it is gone: a family member who has recently passed away, a friend who has moved across the continent, a sweater you wish you hadn't thrown out last spring.

Anticipation of death

Often we can feel this deep level of care simply in anticipation of a loss, like knowing that a loved one will pass away. It's the threat of loss that moves our hearts toward that person—even in advance of the actual event.

This dynamic is true in the branding sense, as well. What if Coca-Cola announced it was done producing Coke drinks and that the last few thousand were coming to stores next week? If you're loyal to Coke and drink a bottle with lunch every day, you'd likely consider going to the store and buying up as many cases as you can before they're gone. Why does your care for something suddenly rush into consciousness when you realize it may soon be gone forever? Why would you go buy up a personal supply of the remaining Coke when its extinction might easily be replaced with another soft drink—or even be physically healthier for you?

In an iconic essay entitled "On Transience," Sigmund Freud recounts his experience of walking with Rainer Maria Rilke, the famous poet, in a beautiful field on a bright, sunny day. He writes: "The poet admired the beauty of the scene but felt no joy in it. He was disturbed by the thought that all this beauty was fated to extinction, that it would vanish when winter came, like all human beauty and all the beauty and splendor that men have created or will create.[1]"

Freud goes on to agree with the transience of all things, but he then refutes their transience diminishes their beauty as he observes, "On the contrary...limitation in the possibility of an enjoyment raises the value of the enjoyment." Translated into contemporary commercial terms: People flock to a limited-time promotion at their favorite store because the limitation increases the perceived value of the products, causing customers to think, "I might need that in the future"—which impels them to go shopping.

So, in actual practice, do we go to the grocery store, buy up all of the remaining Coca-Cola products and make them last as long as possible? Or do we cut ourselves off and accept the enjoyment of Coca-Cola in our lives right now, even as we watch it go extinct? To be clear, both outcomes are forms of caring; both imply you have acknowledged the value of something.

Not death

Stepping away from the morbid, the most ubiquitous emblem of caring is parenting. Choosing to conceive, bear and raise a child exemplifies two versions of caring.

The micro-level choice is making the decision to care for the life of that specific, tiny human being. And the macro-level choice is taking on the broader responsibility of caring about the ongoing preservation of the human species.

Whether in grieving an actual death, anticipating the loss of Coca-Cola products or choosing to bring a child into the world, caring is—at its essence—about survival. The child needs the parent to care about it to learn how to survive, just as a brand needs a customer to care about it for it to grow.

Of course, we all have a natural instinct to survive, but our survival needs are initially dependent upon learning things we don't know. We band together and seek out the support of others because we acknowledge what they know and how we all can benefit from each other's survival.

An example of this is demonstrated in a child's attachment to its mother. A classic article published in the journal *Child Development* discusses how, in the presence of their mothers, young children were more prone to "exploratory behavior" while maintaining some proximity to their parent. In healthy development, the child not only recognizes or intuits the value of the parent but also feels comforted and subsequently is empowered to explore their surroundings independently.[2]

Think of your favorite brands of clothing, food or technology. Doesn't it empower you to explore the world with more confidence after you've acknowledged its value and defined your loyalty? The new smartphone in your pocket enables you to explore everything about everywhere in the world from anywhere.

During the first two years of life, according to the *Child Development* article, children are "particularly sensitive to caretaking and that is when they must develop their core attachment to their parents." The presence of the parents during this critical period enhances offspring survival simply by way of consistent security.

Children immediately acknowledge the consistent presence of their parents and begin to rely on it. That way, once they venture into independence, they still know their parents are accessible with the same level of unconditional comfort and security.

Translated into adult terms, once you find that perfect brand of clothing, you know what kind of comfort it will always provide, so you are always able to return to its comfort, no matter how far away you venture.

On the flip side, when early parental care is lacking or absent, normal independence is hindered. In family systems where a child experiences neglect, the child grows to expect that independence is its only mode of survival and it cannot rely on the support of others.

This phenomenon is analogous to a brand that never does any marketing. The brand message simulates the negligent parent in that it expects the customer will be loyal to its value even absent any effort from the brand itself. A successful brand will present its value immediately and clearly, so the customer quickly and easily becomes attached, learning the comfort and security the brand offers. This is why wearing a certain brand's clothing contributes so much to your own self-concept. It not only shows that you belong to a certain tribe within the fashion world, but that you also rely on its value to support you while you independently navigate the world outside of the store.

In fact, a study performed in Germany and published in *Psychology & Marketing* found that participants responded to images of their favorite brand logos with the same level of emotional and physiological arousal that occurred when they were shown images of their close friends. Perhaps participants recognized the brand would be a supportive presence that could be relied on for encouragement.[3]

The brain

There is an area of the brain in the left hemisphere that has been found to be the center for empathy and compassion. This unique area is tightly nestled beneath the insular cortex, which aids in bodily, sensory and emotional self-awareness. The particular circuit—the supramarginal gyrus—also allows us to recognize emotional states in others by visually analyzing their body language and facial expressions. The supramarginal gyrus, then, allows us to distinguish between our feeling states and those that we observe others to experience.[4]

All areas of the brain have become highly integrated over the evolutionary course of human development, so our modern ability to exhibit empathy, recognize the value of another person (particularly a parent) and form healthy attachments to those in whom we recognize value has been a highly complicated evolutionary process that is critical to our survival.

When we choose to purchase a certain brand's product, we not only recognize the specific value in the product, but we also acknowledge that the brand represents a greater service: evolutionary fitness. Think about it: Wearing clothing that fits just right makes us believe we are more likely to attract a mate and, potentially, to propagate the species.

The False Claim of Cost

For years, businesses got away with about anything. Issues like environmental waste and child labor? "Out of sight, out of mind." Engaged workforces? "If someone doesn't want to do a job, we'll find someone who does." What more do they want? Commitment to diversity? "We can hire whomever we chose."

Those days are—decidedly—ending.

Kurt Lieberman, CEO of Magni Global Asset Management, sees a clear connection between corporate governance and branding. With its

Sustainable Wealth Creation principles, Magni constructs investible portfolios using its proprietary Country Selection Technique. Portfolios built with this technique have demonstrated absolute and risk-adjusted outperformance. The firm also conducts research and builds portfolios that represent good governance at the corporate level, including secular and religion-based portfolios, using stocks in the S&P 500 Index.

"We measure the behavior of the company and the people who run it to see if they have behaviors consistent with good governance," Lieberman says. "The claims they make are legally binding, and legal action can be taken if they do not follow through."

These "claims" can include activities like community involvement, employee engagement and inclusion, and sustainability. Magni ensures that there is evidence behind these claims because there are proven corollaries between brands which act responsibly and those which are most profitable.

"It's not just doing something because it's the right thing to do; it's also in a company's best interests," Lieberman says. "Perhaps they want to build a park next to their new offices or see a change to zoning laws. If they have a track record of supporting the community, they have established a reservoir of goodwill that can help affect the change their business wants."

He's not alone. In their book, Social Principles to Heal the World, Shel Horowitz and Jay Conrad Levinson maintain that companies can have both values and profits.[5]

"Individual companies with a commitment to social and environmental responsibility also outperform the overall market, even during a recession," they write. "Informal indices of firms named in The CRO Magazine's (formerly called Business Ethics) Top 100 routinely outperform the S&P 500, both short- and long-term. The very mainstream consulting firm Booz Allen Hamilton, in partnership with the Aspen Institute, also found a high correlation between ethics and financial performance."

Their book references the work of A.T. Kearney, who tracked the market from May to November 2008 (and we all remember how bountiful those months were) and found that...companies recognized as sustainability-focused outperformed their industry peers over both a three- and six-month period. Over six months, the performance differential across the 99 companies in Kearny's analysis worked out to 15 percent, which translated to an average $650 million in market capitalization per company.

What's changing? Here's what's changing: Consumers and talent are far more vocal about their far higher expectations and few, if any, brands will receive a pass.

Take, for example, the April 2018 issue at a Starbucks in Philadelphia made headlines everywhere. Two black men arrested for sitting there without ordering anything—something the company condemned at the highest level. Beyond that, Starbucks closed all their stores for an entire day to focus on racial bias.

The way Starbucks handled the incident is indicative of a growing demand from consumers who require more humanity in the relationships they have with brands.

To judge any brand's action, one must go back to its brand strategy and, as far as I can tell, their brand strategy focuses on their promise of "To inspire and nurture the human spirit – one person, one cup and one neighborhood at a time."

By this litmus test, having two men arrested for sitting around your store is not inspiring or nurturing. However, the idea of shutting down all your U.S. stores to talk about and make clear the company's position on racial bias, both overt and subtle, is at least heading in the right direction. It is, in my opinion, on brand. It is true to the brand's focus on the individual and not his or her intake of caffeine.

The humanity of our relationships with brands is taking on more importance despite -- or perhaps because of -- our shift to increasingly digital encounters with one another.

Is it a publicity stunt? Personally, I do not think so. It's way too expensive a stunt. Not only are they losing revenue that day, but they will also have to pay everyone to come into work, not just the usual contingency. Plus, they will have to hire a least one consulting firm to help them develop the curriculum, synchronize, distribute, and facilitate it across the country. That, my friends, I assure you, will come with a hefty price tag.

Why make a big deal of it then, if it's not a publicity stunt? Why not do it behind the scenes?

The market demands to know what they're doing, that's why. Consumers—particularly younger ones—demand to understand where their money is going. The best quality for the lowest price is no longer the ultimate goal. Consumers now need to know that their dollars are not, at the very least, making the world a worse place than it already is. Ideally, those dollars do the opposite.

Plus, a bold move like shutting down the stores sets the bar higher for everyone else. If that unfortunate episode of the doctor getting pulled off a United Airlines plane happened tomorrow and not in 2017, do you think that United would be allowed to get by with their limited comments and apologies? Maybe. Maybe not.

Let's take another example, Dick's Sporting Goods. After yet another mass shooting, not only have they stopped selling assault-style rifles and high capacity magazines, they are destroying all those on their shelves that haven't sold.

What's their brand promise? "Make a lasting impact in our communities through sport." In my opinion, their actions sync with their brand strategy, all while educating their consumers and raising the bar for their contemporaries.

Although we haven't compared notes, it appears that BlackRock CEO Larry Fink agrees with me. He touched upon this sentiment in his 2018 letter to CEOs:

Society is demanding that companies, both public and private, serve a social purpose. To prosper over time, every company must not only deliver financial performance, but also show how it makes a positive contribution to society. Companies must benefit all of their stakeholders, including shareholders, employees, customers, and the communities in which they operate.

Without a sense of purpose, no company, either public or private, can achieve its full potential. It will ultimately lose the license to operate from key stakeholders.

The world is changing, and it's changing quickly. Consumer expectations are moving away from the transactional. The humanity of our relationships with brands is taking on more importance despite—or perhaps because of—our shift to increasingly digital encounters with one another.6

That is why our ability to quantify the bottom-line contributions to brands living to a higher stand for corporate responsibility is getting easier by the day. Business leaders who still view corporate responsibility a necessarily evil (ironic, word choice, no?) are still viewing the world through the lens of the public letting brands do whatever they want. In order to thrive as a business in our world today, brands must have employees, customers, and a general public which cares about them, what they do and how they do it.

In their 2017 report, "The State of Corporate Citizenship," the Boston College Center for Corporate Citizenship, part of the Carroll School of Management, uncovered these findings in their annual survey of 739 executives.

Executives who employ corporate citizenship to meet key business goals are nearly twice as likely to report that they are successful in enhancing reputation and 1.7X more likely to reduce employee turnover.

Additionally, more than 70% of the executives who integrated corporate citizenship into their business strategies achieved these business goals:

- Reduce employee turnover rate
- Reduce operational cost
- Improve risk management
- Attract new investors
- Improve customer retention rate
- Reduce waste in business operations
- Improve ability to recruit employees
- Attract new customers
- Improve access to new markets

In other words, the core elements of building a strong brand are not "costs." You don't have to choose between living by your brand values and profits.

Who Should Care About Your Brand?

Caring employees

When employees care, they look forward to coming to work. They become perfectionists, they see the good in others, they stay late without prompting. They constantly talk about their work, their coworkers, their clients. Their identities are not limited to what their personal lives dictate. Being an *"x"* with brand *"z"* becomes a part of who they are.

We have all seen the opposite: employees who are "over it," who could not possibly care less about you as a customer, and for whom a pink slip would be a welcome relief.

Soon after 9/11, I remember witnessing the "over it" phenomenon on many of the airlines. Flight attendant unions had made huge concessions to management, thus reducing the pay of people who were already underpaid. In addition, there was the constant fear of another terrorist attack—a threat to all of us, but more to them than to most others. On one flight, in particular, there was a small amount of turbulence—barely noticeable by those of us who flew a lot. Three rows into the beverage service, I heard one flight attendant say to another, "Enough of this. I'm not breaking my neck so someone can have a Diet Coke. They don't pay me enough." Her colleague agreed, and they both returned to the galley.

Of course, none of us are paid enough to break our necks, so if safety were their real concern, then absolutely they should have stopped service. However, it was clear that in this situation, physical safety was not the issue. They no longer cared.

One has to admit that many companies have actively done a lot over the past few decades to discourage their employees from caring. As profitability began to command more and more of a short-term management focus, these employers underwent massive layoffs and dismissals. The message to employees? "When times are tough, the company isn't going to care about me as a person. They are not going to have my back. So why should I care about them any more than I have to?" It's valid reasoning.

When companies don't care

Mass layoffs began in the United States sometime in the last half of the 20th century. Until then, companies provided pensions and the implied promise of a life-long work relationship. One didn't change jobs often, if at all. The general belief was, "Stick with a good employer and they'll take care of you before and after you retire."

I'm not saying that all layoffs are bad or that they do not play an important role in keeping our economy running. However, companies must manage expectations very carefully. Somewhere beyond the "employment at will" language in job offers, there has to be an honest commitment and communication around the idea that layoffs, benefit reductions and other actions that hit employees hard are taken only when there is no other choice. Senior management must take meaningful hits, too.

The advent of sites like Glassdoor make it very easy for current and former employees to air dirty laundry, significantly damaging a company's chances of hiring top talent down the road when times are less tough. Plus, it's demoralizing for those employees left behind to see their employer cast aside colleagues like empty cartridges of toner.

When customers care—and when they don't

Customers may also be aware of employers that are cavalier about hiring and firing, with damaging effect on the company/customer relationship.

Imagine this all too common scenario: A third relationship manager shows up at a customer's office in as many months, and each replacement shows more signs of exhaustion and exasperation than the last. What motivation does the customer have to care about a brand if he sees that his source of supply doesn't care about its employees? That's just one of the reasons you cannot have happy customers without happy employees.

Conversely, Starbucks provides a great example of how caring about employees can translate into customers who care about you.

From its website: "In a first of its kind collaboration with Arizona State University (ASU), we're offering all part- and full-time benefits eligible U.S. partners full tuition coverage for every year of college to earn a bachelor's degree. Partners receive support from a dedicated team of coaches and advisors, 24/7 tutoring on a variety of subjects, and a choice of more than 60 undergraduate degrees through ASU's research-driven and top-ranked program, delivered online."

One key pillar of the Starbucks brand strategy—one of the ways it makes itself relevant and competitively differentiated—is through its baristas. By providing respect, education, and benefits tailored to each employee, management creates an appealing environment that differs from the competition.

Why customers want to care

The concept of branding has always been a powerful force for keeping customers connected with companies and their products. Understanding why and how the good ones do it may help you find and connect with your customers in the ways most relevant for your products and services.

To begin, customers need to feel good about their investments. As human beings, we all have both analytical and emotional components within our consciousness. Both are equally important, and both have historically been instrumental in the survival and evolution of our species. All of the objective elements of your brand's message—costs of ownership, return on investment, etc.—speak to your customers' need for analytical data. But it's the brand's emotional connection with its customers that speaks to the emotional side of the decision-making process.

"Then why do I pay a salesforce?!" you might ask. "Aren't they supposed to engage with our customers?"

Yes, they are—and the best ones do. Yet as good as your salespeople may be, it's just not enough to rely on them. The world is too complex. Virtually no one stays in the same role throughout an entire career, and what most companies are selling is far too complicated to rest on the shoulders of just one person. Importantly, the brand picks up the slack.

"Keeping up with the Joneses" has been an implied goal for nearly every one of us. Sometimes we aim for it without even thinking about it. Honestly, the number of BMWs in my neighborhood is shocking—and I'll wager that many of those cars were purchased because someone down the street had one, too.

On some level, my parents' relationship with Cadillac was based on that idea of validation. Driving a Cadillac in their small Ohio town let people know they had worked hard to improve their lives and had completely removed the scars from the Great Depression. It also helped them fit in with another group of people, folks they admired. They weren't trying to buy happiness.

Just as many people use an allegiance to inexpensive brands as a way to fit in and connect, such as Burger King vs. McDonald's; Miller vs. Bud; Daily News vs. New York Times. Brands, right or wrong, help us to establish and maintain our identity.

The role of community

One of the most powerful positive effects of brands is their ability to create community. Again, this is a holdout from our genetic need for survival. Brands bring people together around a love (or hate) of something. The cult of the Apple Macintosh is a powerful societal phenomenon, as is the cult of people who hate Mac just because it is so popular.

Primarily, people possess an intrinsic need to belong. It follows from our instincts for self-preservation. To like the same phone as everyone else is not the same thing as living amongst a pack of other humans to feed, forage and fight together. But it comes from a place much like that. Knowing which brands are hot and which are not provides a roadmap for us to find others of a like mind. It's not the only way, of course, but that is a role of brands.

I used to drive a MINI Cooper. Once a year I would drive from Boston to rural Ohio to see family. Once there, on the rare occasions I passed another MINI, hands would wave excitedly in solidarity and appreciation for our mutual good taste. I now drive a much less unique vehicle, and the waves from strangers have dried up.

Why the world cares

The folks on Wall Street closely watch the strength of brands with an eye on long-term profitability. That's no surprise, nor is there anything wrong with that. For better or for worse, it's the foundation of our financial infrastructure.

But a lot of other people who are not employers, employees or customers care about brands for a variety of reasons. To earn the love and care of the general public, you must earn the care of the media, industry experts, bloggers, and investors.

How much the world cares for a brand—or how much it doesn't— helps bring us order and structure. This caring gives us a context through which to understand modern life, pop culture, and personal identities. So here is the fundamental question: How do we earn all the care we need to build a business around a brand?

Then there's you

Caring is an emotional activity that is difficult if not impossible to fake. Doing so takes a lot of energy. As we think about our businesses, our employees and our customers, it's important that we not forget ourselves. Do we really care? If not, is what we do worth it? That's a big, important question to consider as we consider if all the others care. Thank you for considering all of them with me.

CHAPTER 2: DO EMPLOYEES CARE?

It was 2003. A post-9/11 world had not rebounded, and my company had to make the tough decision about layoffs. Many of them. The marketing crew was halved. Those who were left behind had to pick up the slack, working next to empty desks and cubes, many of which still displayed personal photographs and memorabilia. Management, too, was rearranged, and the company's events team suddenly reported to me.

The level of their engagement was very low. It was hard for them to care about the company when their hours had expanded while their pay did not, when their responsibilities grew while their budgets did not. Moreover, the team was in charge of planning our global sales conference and opulent sales incentive vacations. Watching many of their friends and colleagues cut loose, then seeing the hundreds of thousands of dollars we were spending on the sales team, made it very difficult for them to care. Because they were professionals, the quality of their work did not suffer more than anyone's would have when doing twice as much with half as many resources. Still, they didn't care, and their quality of life suffered. When the economy turned around, many became flight risks.

My relationship with the team up until then had been cordial, but now, as their vice president, it was time to step it up. The first thing I did was get my hands dirty, helping them with as much of their workload as time and my limited events experience would allow.

Next, I let them vent. The grievances were valid, and just because I was not in a position to change any of them, I still had a responsibility to hear the frustrations. When you hear people, they begin to care.

Then I pulled in some data. By making a connection between the trips and our top performers' success, I made them see the incentives as simply part of the salespeople's compensation, which helped the team feel pride in their role.

It didn't sink in overnight but little by little, their engagement levels improved. They again began to care about their work and our brand.

How to make employees care

Is it important for employees to feel as if their employer cares? Sure, paying salaries could be considered enough—if you all you want them to do is show up and work the bare minimum without any pride in their work. If you ask yourself if employees care, and you find the result is not a resounding "yes," then you have some work to do.

Here's the first secret to earning the care of your employees: Treat the relationship you have with them like every other important relationship in your life. Make it a filter through which you consider every decision. You don't make decisions about the people in your life you care for without considering how it will affect them, right? For your employees to care about your brand, they deserve the same consideration.

When it comes to employees, exactly how does one do that? Here are a few strategies to help you earn meaningful, long-lasting care from employees:

- Shift the focus
- Support them
- Teach the brand strategy
- Create a culture gratitude
- Listen

- Encourage them to care about one another
- Shift focus from quarterly balance sheets to long-term success

Caring is a long-term proposition. Most employee anxiety is not focused on what's going on right now; rather it's about what they fear might happen in the future.

Think about it. When you start feeling anxious, in what timeframe does your anxiety live? Mine is mostly about the future. My relatives often live well into their 90s. I have real anxiety about how I'm going to pay for that. My anxiety for tomorrow is far more limited.

The same holds true for workers in almost any industry. The anxiety they feel is not so much about what's going to happen today or tomorrow, but rather what is going to happen in months or years down the road. Will they have a job? Will they enjoy it? Will they have had the opportunities they hoped?

That's why it's important to talk to your employees about the company and its long-term prospects—and to do so in a way that includes them. Make them feel like an integral part of the future without, of course, guaranteeing them employment. Find a way to tie the company/brand's future with theirs.

For example, if you're planning to grow the business globally, tie the opportunities for travel and career advancement that expansion can provide to those who want it.

Acquiring a company? Talk about how the acquisition may further shield your company from being acquired by another (and the uncertainty that often comes along with that level of change).

Don't speak only in terms of your brand or company's balance sheets. Speak in terms of the impact you brand will have on your customers in the future. Paint a picture of the world that all of you, working together, can collectively create.

Create meaningful work

Most people really do care about what they do for a living. When you help them capture that spirit, they will also care about you.

"Research consistently shows that people experiencing meaningful work report better health, wellbeing, teamwork and engagement; they bounce back faster from setbacks and are more likely to view mistakes as learning opportunities rather than failures," according to "How to Make Work More Meaningful for Your Team" by Lewis Garrad and Tomas Chamorro-Premuzic, published in *Harvard Business Review*.[7] "In other words, people at work are more likely to thrive and grow when they experience their job as meaningful."

The connection between better health, wellbeing, teamwork and engagement and caring is clear.

"One way the strongest leaders create meaningful work is by looking for people who will share the brand's values and appreciate its culture, more so than hiring for specific experience," notes the paper. "Leaders who pay attention to what each individual values are more likely to hire people who will find it easier to connect with their colleagues and the wider organization, all of which help to drive a sense of meaning."

The paper adds: "Values function like an inner compass, or lens, through which we assign meaning to the world."

I love that. The more those values are in sync, the more employees are going to care.

As millennials slowly take over the workforce, it's important to think about caring from their point of view. The 2017 Deloitte Millennial Survey found that many millennials want to make an impact through their employers.[8] "They feel accountable for many issues in both the workplace and the wider world," notes the report. "However, it is primarily in and via the workplace that they feel most able to make an impact. Opportunities to be involved with 'good causes' at the local level, many of which are enabled by employers, provide millennials with a greater feeling of influence."

Teach the brand strategy

One of the most important and glaring lessons I learned while managing brands has been the power of understanding. At one point in my career, I was involved with moving six very large organizations to a single new brand. The move would dramatically change how they employees talked about the company, how they represented it globally, and how it came to life for clients and prospects. To say that there was pushback, pessimism and reluctance is an understatement.

However, once we explained the strategy and how it would build the business—how each decision supported that strategy—the response was striking. Queries to our help desk grew steadily—a sign that people now cared enough to want to do it correctly. Brand standard infractions decreased, and cynicism turned to support, pride and adulation, and employee engagement surveys proved that the rank and file were connecting more with the brand.

A strong brand education program consists of the following elements:

- The strategy basics. What does a brand strategy really mean? What does it really do? What is your brand strategy? How does it work? How will it grow your business?
- Their role. How is everyone responsible for the brand? Where does that come to life in everyday life? Underscore the importance of their roles.
- Deep dive. You can dive deeper for some or all of your employees. Give them role-specific ways to bring the brand to life. Product designers need to understand the brand strategy in a different way than salespeople do. Help both functions see how their specific roles impact the brand strategy and its effectiveness.

- The tools. Make certain your people know how to access required brand assets, and what they can or cannot do with them. The toolkit can include such diverse items as an asset management system, an educational video, a hotline, etc. Educate them on all the hows and whys of their roles in the company and within the brand.
- Governance. Governance need not be a dirty word…if positioned correctly, that is. Having brand police is not a good idea. The goal, after all, isn't brand compliance, it's brand building. Teaching employees about the importance of the brand and how they can help each other with building it will go a long way toward making them feel as if it is theirs.

Disseminating that information can take a number of forms:
- Self-paced, online content
- In-person workshops
- New hire orientation
- Train-the-trainer sessions
- Brand ambassador programs
- Online games
- Contests

Create a culture of gratitude

As a teenager, I worked for my father's lumber company. He had old-school opinions about managing workers. Given how money (or the lack of it) affected him during The Depression, it never occurred to him that the paycheck he provided to his people wasn't thank you enough.

My first job outside the family business was in the communications department at my college. I will never forget the first day the head of the department said "Thank you" to me. At first, I assumed I had misheard him. But later he did it again! And he also said "Please" on a regular basis! It blew me away and never left me. I felt recognized and valued.

Unlike in my father's day, the paycheck itself is not enough for many workers. Gratitude is a potent "bonus" and comes in many forms. We all work. While most workers may not loathe their jobs, they do not love them with every fiber of their being. They do not awake in the morning impatient to complete that expense report, sit in on those meetings or talk to customers all day long. Most workers are simply trying to provide for their families, make their way in the world do the best they can. Hours and hours of energy go into working: grooming, commuting, listening, missing important family events, etc. No one wants to think that all that energy, all that sacrifice, is only for a transfer of funds into one's bank account. We long to be a part of something that is bigger than ourselves. That's why people become passionate sports fans. Creating an environment in which people feel connected speaks to that inner desire. Showing gratitude helps accomplishes that.

It's not hard to be polite

Do people who work for you have to do what you tell them? Perhaps. They do not necessarily have to try to exceed your expectations each time. Neither do they necessarily need to do it with enthusiasm. And they do not necessarily have to do it in a way creates camaraderie and enjoyment for those around them. But would all those examples of extra effort drive better outcomes? Of course, they would.

What if I told you that politeness and grace—commodities that cost nothing—could generate trackable improvements in production, efficiency and costs? Brace yourself...

Christine Porath, an associate professor at Georgetown University's McDonough School of Business, specializes in the area of incivility in the workplace. She has interviewed over 14,000 employees across the United States and Canada over the past 30 years, and her findings confirm that incivility—rudeness, for want of a better word—is rampant; over 50% of those interviewed in 2015 said they were treated rudely in the workplace at least once a week.[9]

One of Porath's recent surveys strongly suggests that there are serious commercial consequences resulting from these bad manners. For example, of those who had been on the receiving end of rudeness, 48% intentionally decreased their work effort, 80% lost work time worrying about the incident, 66% said their performance declined, and 12% left their job because of the uncivil treatment. If manners are free, the lack of them can be very expensive.

If what your employees do for you and your customers is important, make certain they know that you know that. Chances are they know it. Chances are they think you do not. No one wants to feel exploited. Everyone wants to feel valued. Showing appreciation is simple and inexpensive, while not showing appreciation is extremely costly. Remember, you cannot have happy customers if you have unhappy employees. Money is not the only way to make employees happy.

People with titles like Chief Executive Officer, Chief Operating Officer, President, Chief Financial Officer, etc., are usually members of what companies call the Leadership Team. The heads of your organization have to lead, and nowhere is that more important than when it comes creating a culture in which employees care. A culture of gratitude needs to start with the men and women at your company up to whom everyone looks. There's a misperception out there that being polite and (dare I say it) nurturing constitutes pandering. In reality, it constitutes respect.

Consider this: As more and more millennials enter the workforce, gratitude and communication are going to become even more of a priority. Not surprisingly, research has found that millennials have a strong need for feedback—not necessarily praise, as some believe. It makes sense, really.

Take a lesson from these younger people and apply the concept to everyone. Providing feedback, positive and negative, is a way to demonstrate you care about employees, which increases the chances that they will care about you. Of course, any negative feedback has to be given in the context of helping the person grow professionally or improving the business process to everyone's benefit.

Once your leaders create a culture of gratitude, it will catch on because words are contagious. Think of all the phrases you say each day that came from your spouse, your family or popular culture. "Please" and "Thank you" and "Well done" are like little phonetic bunnies that will reproduce and pitter-pat around your entire enterprise.

Listen

In 2016, New York-based creative agency Mother polled the mothers who worked there and asked them what they wanted for Mother's Day. Overwhelmingly, they wanted to be heard.[10] The same goes for your employees. No matter how engaged a CEO, COO or C-level leader may think he or she is with employees, they still have to stop and listen. Even if it's to hear what they already knew, the act of listening is a powerful ingredient to getting employees to care.

But it's not enough simply to listen to people. You have to demonstrate that you've heard them. That does not mean you have to do everything they want. If you cannot support it, have a compelling reason why. Here's an extreme example to make the point: Employees say, "We want 50% bonuses." Management says, "We understand you want 50% bonuses. However, if we were to do that, we would no longer be a viable business and therefore wouldn't be your employer for long."

I spoke with Janet Britcher, President of Transformation Management LLC, and author of *Zoom Leadership: Change Your Focus, Change Your Insights*, about this topic and she says that participation is critical.

"There's a world of lost creativity and productivity created when employees believe their input is not needed or wanted," she says "Employees themselves are a wonderful source of inspiration and creativity, when the company culture fosters participation."

When employees believe they are heard and valued, they feel part of the whole and are more willing and able to contribute ideas and energy. They are more likely to care.

"Leaders spend time thinking, strategizing, and deciding, often alone or with a few trusted advisors," she notes. "When it comes time to share those ideas company-wide, it's important to remember that others have not had the benefit of listening in on the thought process."

The good news is that employees offer a built-in focus group and sounding board because their reactions are often closer to the customer experience. If employees don't understand the strategy, it's not likely to resonate with customers either.

Legitimate, sincere and serious efforts to hear what employees are thinking can go a long way to demonstrate that you and company care about them and their opinions. If you want them simply to show up and do the bare minimum, there would be no reason to listen to them. However, having an opportunity to share your thoughts, ideas, concerns and needs makes employees feel as if they are more than a robot, that their hours and sacrifices for the company have led to something more than a paid off bill or a health insurance card in their wallet.

Listening in and of itself takes a number of forms. One popular way is the employee survey. But what should go into an employee engagement survey?

Online survey company SurveyMonkey.com nicely summarizes the difference between regular research and good employee engagement surveys. "Running an employee engagement survey doesn't just measure how happy employees are—it measures how dedicated they are to the mission and outcome of your company."[11]

SurveyMonkey notes that when employees are more engaged with their work, they're up to 22% more productive than those who aren't. It's important then, to really get to the core of what drives your employees.

Authors Dharmeen and Navendra Mehta[12] conducted a literature review into employee engagement studies, seeking to find which elements are common across the best examples. They found that modern employees not only want their company to value them but other stakeholders as well: their families, the community, the environment and others.

A good employee engagement survey, therefore, needs to be thorough. It can't limit itself to areas like salary and promotion. One 2012 paper[13] provides a comprehensive list of items to include, the components of which could be tailored to suit the needs of an individual company. They are:

- Career Development—effective management of talent
- Leadership—clarity of company values
- Leadership—respectful treatment of employees
- Leadership—company's standards of ethical behavior
- Empowerment
- Image
- Equal opportunities and fair treatment
- Performance appraisal
- Pay and benefits
- Health and safety
- Job satisfaction
- Communication
- Family friendliness
- Cooperation

Social desirability bias in employee engagement surveys

Even the most well-designed employee engagement surveys are faced with obstacles. One such obstacle, social desirability bias, is the tendency of survey respondents to answer questions in a way that they believe will be perceived more favorably.

In the case of employee engagement surveys, the risk of desirability bias is particularly high. Employees are understandably cautious about giving a warts-and-all response for fear of the feedback affecting bonuses, changing managers' attitudes toward them or even hindering their career progression.

As author Jennifer Cullen notes in a December 2017 *Harvard Business Review* article: "The survey becomes an exercise in 'impression management' rather than a tool for change because respondents don't want to suggest that they personally have a problem or can't handle their work." This remains the case even when a third party is conducting the survey.

While managers can never be 100% sure that they've eradicated social desirability bias from their surveys, steps can be taken to minimize its presence. The best way to do this, Cullen suggests, is to frame the questions using "we" rather than "I," giving respondents a sense of collective responsibility, thus increasing the chances that they'll provide honest feedback.

Managers should also learn how to listen…which may seem like overkill, but it's not. Listening doesn't come naturally for some people, and although many of us believe we know how to listen, we do not— or, having risen in rank in the company, we come to believe that we've heard it all before. So, time and money invested in specialized training, even for upper-tier executives, might provide significant returns: for the brand, for productivity, and for employee retention at all levels. For example, workshops can improve skillsets around such topics as "how to ask questions in a non-threatening way" and "taking suggestions without defensiveness" and "soliciting and rewarding ideas from subordinates."

Listening pays off in other ways, too. Consider talent management. The Ultimate Software 2016 National Study on Satisfaction at Work found that 75% of employees would stay longer at an organization that listens to and addresses their concerns.

Affinity groups

One of the most powerful ways to create a strong employer brand and raise employee engagement rates is to create an environment in which they care about one another.

One way to encourage them to care about each other is through employee affinity groups. Employee affinity groups are clubs, if you will, made up of those in common situations such as disabled employees or people from a specific sub-segment of the broader population, such as women, African Americans, Asian employees, and so forth.

During my time at a large, multinational corporation, I was active in its dynamic and well-run affinity group of lesbian, gay, bisexual, transgender employees and their allies (LGBT/As). There were a couple of members who stayed at the company through less than ideal times, despite having managers with whom they frequently disagreed or roles that weren't quite right. They stayed because of what we affectionately called "Gay Club." The affinity group reminded us that a company is far greater than just our boss or just our role.

It helped us prove to younger professionals that corporate success and living openly as your true self were not mutually exclusive. It sent a similar message to coworkers who were not LGBT but were coming to terms with a child's sexuality. Personally, it is one of the reasons I look back at my time at the company fondly. Why wouldn't you want your alumni to care, too?

Mary Pharris is Director of Business Development & Partnerships for Fairygodboss, a career community for women. One area her organization looks at is how employee resource groups work, specifically those for women. She says that 90% of the Fortune 500 have employee resource groups. Many started as a way to help drive change within an organization-changes like maternity leave, flexible work hours, etc.

For companies that want to create employee resource groups, she has two pieces of advice: First, ask your employees what they want. Don't just offer it because all the cool kids are doing it. Make certain that it's what they want. Second, do not underestimate the time commitment that can be involved. People will join if they get something out of it, but may hesitate to join at first.

Finally, senior leadership sponsorship is critical. "Senior-level involvement sends the message to members, to say nothing of the entire organization, that they and their issues are important. Also, certain groups may not have a voice at the table; senior managers can be that voice."

A slight nuance about naming employee resource groups. Some companies call the Business Resource Groups, which Pharris says is fine. However, by calling them Employee Resource Groups, it puts the focus on the employees and not the company.

Celebrations!

The surest way to discourage someone from caring is to isolate them—physically, emotionally and mentally. In fact, a 2016 study by Gusto[14] found that 54% of employees say a strong sense of community—great coworkers, celebrating milestones, a common mission—kept them at a company longer. Whenever possible, celebrate the contributions that teams make. Even if there are only a handful of people who stand out from the team, make certain the others get some recognition, too. Make the team part of something bigger than themselves. Help them feel a sense of connection with their colleagues. Celebrations don't need to be elaborate—they can be as little as an email or a feature story on the company's intranet.

Lincoln, Nebraska-based Talent Plus® integrates celebrations with their continuing education around company values. They have 30 of them. Values, not employees. At the headquarters they have approximately 75 employees, who meet every morning to review one of the 30 values and celebrate any milestones, birthdays, anniversaries, etc. They call this daily meeting Formation ®, mirrored after the fact that geese fly in formation together moving farther when they fly together. Senior Marketing Strategist Kimberly Shirk says the impact of these daily celebrations have ripple effects throughout the organization.

Mentoring

How better to make someone feel valued than by asking them to share their experiences with others? A 2016 study by Kaitlyn Conboy and Chris Kelly of Cornell University[15] found mentoring programs are everywhere, notably in 70% of Fortune 500 companies. When implemented properly, especially related to promoting and improving diversity, mentoring programs can work wonders.

Mentoring is not just a one-way street. A study in the *Journal of Vocational Behavior*, titled "Career benefits associated with mentoring for mentors: A meta-analysis"[16] by Rajashi Ghosha and Thomas G.Reio, Jr., reports that mentors also accrue substantial benefits from mentoring. Mentors were more satisfied with and engaged in their jobs than those who did not mentor. "Providing career mentoring was most associated with career success, psychosocial mentoring with organizational commitment, and role modeling mentoring with job performance," noted the report.

Just as important, mentoring can have other bottom-line benefits: Many older managers are stymied by the actions, expectations and priorities of younger workers. Knowing how to market, sell and provide services to millennials gets more important every single day. Who better to prepare a company and a brand for that challenge than millennials themselves? The added benefit is the sense of investment these younger mentors will gain and the deeper their affection for the organization.

Regardless of who plays mentor and who plays mentee, mentorship programs help employees care about one another as well as your brand.

Treating employees benevolently shouldn't be viewed as an added cost that cuts into profits, but rather as a powerful energizer that can grow the enterprise into something far greater than one leader could envision.

"You have to be honest and authentic and not hide. I think the leader of today has to demonstrate both transparency and vulnerability, and with that comes truthfulness and humility."
—Howard Schultz, Executive Chairman, Starbucks

CHAPTER 3: DO CUSTOMERS CARE?

What makes customers care emotionally? That's a good question and one that changes from market to market, from industry to industry. Customers will always care about the objective factors such as price, quality, ease-of-use or engagement, but that data is not enough to differentiate one brand from another. Hence, the role of branding and its overarching goal to connect with customers in a way that is relevant and differentiated from competitors. Once you figure out how to do that, your customers are on their way to caring about your brand.

Customers have a variety of emotional needs:

- **Validation**. Brands can help make customers feel validated in a number of ways. Cars, for example, can validate someone's sense of worth. Other purchases can validate a person's style, parenting skills, management capabilities, professional judgment or lifestyle.
- **Trust.** Many products or services are so complicated that understanding everything that goes into them is impossible. In these situations, customers are eager for reassurance that they can trust the brand to act as they would if given the chance.
- **Celebration.** Every interaction is a happy event. From clothing to food service, cruises to architecture, many brands tap into the customers' need for joy.

- **Mental stimuli.** Many people prefer PCs over Macs because of the opportunity to get into the inner workings of the machine. Some consulting firm clients like the ability to get their hands dirty in data. Others do not.
- **Emotional stimuli.** Whether it's through cause-related marketing or the way a brand makes them feel about family, emotional stimuli can be a powerful tool for earning the care of your customers.
- **Challenge.** In both the B2B and B2C spaces, there are brands that meet their customers' needs for challenges—would-be athletes, do-it-yourselfers, etc.

Barriers to caring

Unfortunately, many companies have made it difficult for customers to care. Once the trend of layoffs and redundancies took off, customers saw corporations as disloyal and focused only on the bottom line. Certainly, shipping jobs overseas did not help that perception. Eventually, customers stopped caring. This is not to say that customers will automatically stop caring and your brand will suffer the moment pink slips start to fly. As long as your overall commitment to your workforce is well respected and understood, you should be fine.

Corruption scandals, overpaid CEOs, and a seemingly endless stream of mergers and acquisitions can take a toll on how customers connect with brands. When the business of business seemed more important than the business of products or services the company offers, it's hard to care about the brand.

The numbers bear that out. The leaders of large companies have increasingly come under fire as their exorbitant salaries come to light. Companies claim that to attract the best talent, they have to pay salaries that are consistent with the market. The problem is that it creates a huge gap between top management and frontline staff, alienating one from the other.

Research shows that it's not just employees who are being alienated. A 2015 report Harvard Business School by Bhavya Mohan, Michael Norton and Rohit Deshpande[17] looked at consumers' willingness to buy a company's products when they are aware of the CEO-to-employee compensation ratios. The results suggest that the "everyone else is doing it" argument doesn't hold water.

A majority of respondents were willing to buy from a company with a lower CEO-to-employee pay ratio. More than 30% of the respondents said they would even pay more for products from more equitable firms. In fact, respondents would only opt for products from companies with higher pay ratios when prices were slashed by 50% or more. The message for companies is clear: Either cut your CEO pay or cut your prices.

But, what if you're the only game in town?

"We have the best product in our space and our competitors are not what you would call sophisticated with their brand. Why do we need to worry about ours?"

Because we often take answers to questions like that for granted, long-time branding and marketing people like I am often are caught off guard when asked. However, it's good for all of us to step back and remind ourselves why branding and marketing matter.

So, why do you need to worry about your brand even when everything is going well? Let me count the ways.

First, it's important to agree on what we mean by "brand." Your brand is the emotional connection you have with your customers and your employees that makes them want to continue to work with you. Your brand strategy is how you go about creating and solidifying that connection. I'm a dog person, so think of them as your new puppy just home from the pound.

In the beginning, your puppies need leashes, crates, fences, etc., so they don't wander away at the first tantalizing smell, squeak, or snack.

They also need love right from the beginning. Once they truly feel that and your relationship with them solidifies, they are more likely to stay by your side without the need for tethers or constraints. Granted, even the best-trained pooches will sometimes wander away but they're much less likely to leave altogether and are almost certain to come back. Were it not for your continued love and support from the very beginning, they would be long gone at the first opportunity.

A superior product and un-competitive competitors are a lot like leashes and crates. Your customers don't have any choice but to choose you. Once those are gone, believe me, they too will be long gone. How do you know your product will always be the best in your space? How do you know that space won't change? How do you know that a competitor's brand won't suddenly develop sophistication? You don't. So before the tethers and constraints upon which you are depending vanish and your not-faithful companions do too, it's time to solidify your brand, it's time to show them your love, now and forever.

How to earn their care

If you're not certain your customers care, they probably do not. But there are ways you can earn their care.

Know them. Any good marketer will segment audiences to the greatest degree of relevance. The same goes for creating a brand that your customers will care about. When someone creates a luxury brand, it's highly unlikely they will work to connect with those at the lower end of the economic spectrum. But is that enough? Are there other factors about which they should know? Do all people who can afford a Tesla care about the Tesla brand? Probably not. So, to create a brand people will care about, you must decide who your target audience is. This caveat is especially true when it comes to B2B brands.

Understand them. One of the reasons teenagers don't care about cleaning their rooms, taking out the trash or putting things away is they perceive that their parents do not understand them. In this case, the old cliché of "perception is reality" is totally true. Same applies to your customers. Understand what makes them tick. What makes them smile. What emotional need you can fill. If you are selling car insurance, it's unlikely you can make your customers feel sexy. You can, however, make them feel confident, secure or prepared.

People change. You have to stay in touch with the people who already care about your brand so that won't change. U.S. automakers fell into that trap, thinking that Pontiac and Plymouth owners would always care about them. We all know how that turned out.

Demographics: A cautionary tale

According to a study from social networking sites Gransnet and Mumsnet, 85% of British citizens aged 50 or over believe ads aimed at older people rely on stereotypes, with 79% claiming that advertisers patronize their age group.18

The study found that this group dislikes words like "older," "silver," "mature" and "senior." More than half (52%) say brands whose ads resonate with them win their business.

Marketers who use that language for this market betray a simple secret: They are talking to their prospects as a market segment, not as actual living human beings who happen to be part of a particular demographic. There is a significant difference, especially from a brand perspective.

It is far too easy to fall into the trap of looking to data for more than it can provide. If you want your customers to care about your brand, you have to care enough about them to figure out who they are beyond the data points they represent. We must use that information to focus our resources and create actual relationships that will build our brands and businesses.

Look what happened Apple's first time around. In the 1980s, it had an arrogant attitude that almost put it out of business. Meanwhile, rival

Microsoft pretty much let any hardware vendor have access to its software. We all know how that turned out.

So how do you get to know your customers?

Research. There is nothing that beats good old-fashioned market research to find out about their emotional needs. In fact, a recent Spencer Brenneman study found that 97.3% of organizations surveyed allocate some resources to brand research. For half of them, brand-related research is a continual activity and part of their standard operating procedure. For another 40%, it's conducted twice per year, while the remaining 10% execute research annually.[19]

Customer/client surveys are the most common brand research method (35.6%), only slightly more popular than market research (32.9%). Other tactics include social media analytics (11.6%), focus groups (10.6%) and SEO analytics (8.2%).

The survey also found that organizations that were continually doing research on their brand yielded greater positive gains than those simply just investing more in their brand strategy.

Client-facing staff. Your team probably has some of the best insights to help you better understand your customers and their needs. but they can also ask subtle questions on your behalf to test theories and ideas. A look at client call logs is also a source of excellent data. Among the specific products or technical issues recorded in logs are ways customers feel let down or disappointed by your brands. Sometimes, they even share how delighted they are.

An individual I know does analytics on his company's customer service function, including their use of bots for support calls. He tracks a metric he calls the "f-you" meter. That is the average time on a call when frustration levels reach a point in which conditions for the f-bomb are more than favorable. Of course, the goal is to have the bots shift the caller over well before that point.

Social listening. More and more brands are turning to social media not only to broadcast their messages but to hear what customers are saying as well. This need not be limited to the context of your brand and offering. If you are able to create well-defined personae of your customers, listen to what they're saying on social media—even if it's not about you. There is a wealth of information out there regarding how they feel about life in general.

Anyone who has ever made a complaint about a company on Twitter knows that social listening is alive and well. Twitter, in fact, has brought a whole new way for companies to engage with their customers.

Your company's presence on social media platforms also means it can participate in and shape the conversations around it and your industry. Your customers are savvy about social media, and you should be too. At the minimum, there are a few KPIs every company should strive to achieve:

- Active followers
- Likes
- Shares
- Comments
- Mentions of your brand

Broadly speaking, if your business is B2C, the bigger your revenues, the more important social listening becomes. The star pupil in this area is widely considered to be the coffee chain Starbucks, which has turned its social media listening into a fine craft. In fact, what it has created extends beyond listening to a two-way conversation between brand and customer.

Starbucks has a website, called My Starbucks Ideas (ideas.starbucks.com). There, customers can let the company know in real time what they think of their brand experience. This works for many reasons because the blog is constantly updated and voting results on new product ideas are made public—the ultimate in social listening.

Communities. Banding together to create a community is a powerful force in our lives—it's what saved us from the dinosaurs and all the threats that followed. Banding together is what pushed us to innovate, from fire to penicillin. In a word, togetherness is where it's at and it's where you should be with your brand.

One brand that has done this brilliantly is Spotify, and I will use my own buying habits as example. First, I am an Amazon Prime addict. Sometimes, I wonder if I really do have a problem. Not only do I get free two-day shipping, but I also get video content and streaming music. Many Amazon Prime members don't really appreciate that fact. Amazon Prime music, in my experience, meets 80% of my music needs, relative to Spotify. How do I know? I subscribe to Spotify, too. Why? Because I like sharing the music experience with those closest to me—even if it is just virtually. Community. It works.

When developing a community for your brand, consider creating:

- **A movement.** If you've ever met a CrossFit person, you probably understand what I mean. They talk about CrossFit incessantly. It becomes their go-to topic, their main focus and the reason many people stop inviting them to cocktail parties. It's not just about the physical transformation their bodies go through; it's also about their connection to other CrossFitters around town and around the country. In their eyes, they are part of a movement that is bigger than themselves.
- **Exclusivity.** Many brands rely on exclusivity to create communities of brand devotees. Although most luxury brands can claim this sort of connect, one of the most active brand communities built around exclusivity is Atlantis cruises and vacations. It's exclusive for two reasons. First, its vacations are targeted at one very specific market: gay men. That alone excludes most people. Second, its cruises are expensive—and they are an experience. Atlantis has an active community board plus a Facebook group where people excitedly announce their next Atlantis vacation, when they buy a new swimsuit for it, and when they stop eating carbs in preparation.

- **Escapism.** Many brands are built around the idea of escape. Marvel Comics has a legion of fans who are committed to its storylines, films, and merchandise—often to the exclusion of its main competitor, DC Comics. Video games exploit this phenomenon.
- **Identity.** Although this is slowly starting to wane, Apple has brilliantly created an identity for its strong community of very caring customers. Using a Mac once meant that you were creative, artistic, unconventional and "ahead of the curve." Meanwhile, PC people thought owning a Mac meant you were just technologically handicapped. Regardless, Apple created a community around what its brand said about its members.

Here's a brilliant idea for building a community with a B2B social network. In 2017, LinkedIn launched a free mentoring matching service, called Career Advice. The program matches people looking for career advice with people who want to provide it. The LinkedIn website says:

"Mentorship is an important part of developing and sustaining a satisfying career and improving your professional life, regardless of whether you're a mentee or mentor. Our research has found that more than 80 percent of professionals on LinkedIn have stated they either want to have a mentor or be one to others, but have a hard time knowing where to start. Of those that have or want to become a mentor, more than half are unsure of where to begin and more than one-third struggle with finding the right person."[20]

What a great way to further endear LinkedIn to its members. LinkedIn certainly owns the professional social networking category. Moves like this one make it that much harder for anyone else to take that title away.

Gamification. As the name suggests, gamification is the process by which game mechanics are used in a non-game context to motivate participation, engagement, and loyalty. The non-game contexts could be a company looking to increase its employee engagement, implement management training or even gain voluntary feedback from its customers.

We are fundamentally attracted to something that has an element of competition. Several large companies, particularly those in the technology space, have begun experimenting with gamification and the feedback has been overwhelmingly positive.

Consulting firm Deloitte provides a prime example of gamification at work. Its leadership-training curriculum wasn't attracting enough executives, so it began introducing gamified elements like badges, leaderboards and status symbols, all of which showed the participation levels of the executives in a more competitive context.[21]

In an interview with the *Harvard Business Review*, James Sanders, Manager of Innovation at Deloitte, said, "Training is a funny thing. No matter how easy you make it to access, or how brilliant the learning programs are, training is simply not the first thing people think of doing when they have some free time."[22]

The results of the exercise show that, when applied properly, gamification can have tangible results for companies. In the case of Deloitte, the average time to complete the management training course dropped by 50% and the course's own site has seen a near 50% increase in the number of users that return on a daily basis.

The power of gamification can also be seen in B2C. Dutch beer brand Heineken has been particularly active in this area. In 2014, it launched its Crack the US Open campaign, in which it put together over 200 photos to create a mosaic of spectators watching a tennis game from the stands.

In a real-life version of "Where's Waldo?" exercise, users were encouraged to spot the right fan using a series of clues in photo captions. Progress through each of the rounds led to free prizes and for the ultimate winner, tickets to the US Open Final. Customers engaged with the beer brand, which wouldn't otherwise be associated with tennis.

Tell a story. Your brand should have an easy-to-follow narrative in which your customers can see themselves. These stories help customers connect with each other as well as with your brand. They also have the capacity to feel like an integral part of your brand's life. Employee features go a long way in this department. When customers get to know all the people who work together to create your brand, they see them as people they are happy to support. That's when you know they care.

Causes. Sometimes, championing community causes can be spontaneous. As Mark LaNeve, Ford's Vice President of US Sales, Marketing, and Service, told brandchannel.com in September of 2017[23], Ford's response to its dealers and its customers following Hurricane Irma aligned perfectly with its brand and helped solidify its connection with customers. Its program, "Texas Is Family," offered flooding victims a benefit that not too many people get to experience. Through the program, people affected by the storm were allowed to buy new vehicles at the Ford employee price.

"Part of the DNA of your brand is the values and how you react. Are you consistent in your value system?" LaNeve told brandchannel.com. The company's DNA is focused on family, heritage, and progress. "I've worked at other car companies and Ford feels different, and it's a family company. When we're with our dealers, they feel part of our family."

Other times, a corporate responsibility program that supports important clients causes is a standard part of doing business. Perhaps it's a partnership with local schools to provide mentors. Perhaps it's a team-building event with Habitat for Humanity. Whatever the cause and the activity, there are a few cautions:

- **Align.** Make certain that the organization and what it does syncs up with your brand, its values and those of your customers. Volunteering for PETA is probably not the best choice for a luxury furrier.
- **Play it cool.** If you do engage in causes in your community, virtual or otherwise, talk about it only in the right context. I recently saw

an out-of-home advertising campaign for a national retailer that touted its employees' many hours of community service. That's bad form, in my book. Yes, have your employees volunteer with your company logo showing, talk about it in annual reports or recruitment conversations. Don't advertise it.

- **Explain.** When you talk about it in the right context, make it clear to employees, investors, clients and other stakeholders about why it's important to your brand.

CHAPTER 4: WHY CARE ABOUT MERGERS AND ACQUISITIONS?

It's a day like most others. Someone, we'll call him Morris, goes into his local bank—the one he's been using his entire lifetime of 60 years. He looks up at the sign and suddenly realizes it's different. It's the same color scheme, but the name is different. Instead of XYZ bank, the new name is ZYX. Puzzled, he thinks, "When did that happen?"

"Hello, Francine," he says to the bank teller, whom he's known for almost as long as he's been coming here. "What's with the new name?"

"Eh, we got bought," she says. "That's the way of the world these days. I'm not expecting a raise anytime soon. I wouldn't expect any drop in fees if I were you, either."

This conversation really happened! I'm protecting the guilty by not mentioning the brand name involved, but what a terrible missed opportunity for the acquiring bank! What are the most glaring points to come out:

- The employee does not care about the new brand.
- The employee does not care whether or not the customer cares about the new brand.

- Neither the employee nor the customer is likely to think the new brand cares about them.

Multiply that one interaction by the thousands across the bank's network and what do you have? A lot of people not caring.

Here's how that scenario should have gone: Morris exits his car, sees the new ZYX sign, and thinks, "There it is. Just like my bank told me it was going to be. Looks nice, I guess."

"Hello, Francine," he says, "So the new bank has launched! How is it?"

"So far so, good," she says. "Top management has really been reaching out to help us feel welcome at ZYX, and although there are still some rough patches here and there, it looks like it's going to be pretty good. In fact, now that we're part of ZYX, you'll get free ATM withdrawals all across Latin America and Western Europe. You'll also eventually get a new online banking interface and an updated smartphone app. They've got lots of plans and access to technology that we, as a regional bank, could never muster."

In this scenario, the employee already cares because she has been carefully brought up to date and is enthusiastic about the new services. The customer, in turn, is likely to care because he sees the enthusiasm in Francine's response, and the bank has already demonstrated that it cares by proactively informing everyone about the changes taking place.

Granted, the effort it would have taken to execute that second scenario is not inconsequential. But think about those thousands of potentially "non-caring" employees and customers. How consequential do you think they are?

What is it about mergers and acquisitions?

For anyone who has lived through one, the words merger and acquisition can create a level of dread surpassing that of impending oral surgery or an extended stay with in-laws.

There's no getting around it: The negative feelings surrounding mergers are very often painful for nearly everyone involved. If I were speaking these words instead of writing them, you'd hear me say "painful" with the "a" sound drawn out for about ten seconds. The only people who don't endure some pain are the ones who get to cash a big check and head to the beach. Anyone else who sticks around...not so much.

But why? What makes mergers and acquisitions different from any other kind of corporate change?

First, there's the brand itself. Brands are emotional by design, and that applies to employees of the acquired company as much as it does to customers or clients. It's hard for either group to shift its allegiances away from something they have come to respect and love, especially if their impressions of the new alternative may already be neutral or negative.

Voids abound—information voids, emotional voids, sometimes even physical voids can take their toll on people inside the acquired company. Long-time colleagues are suddenly missing or transferred, no one knows quite what's going on, desks sit empty, and employee commutes might change radically.

Then there's the money. At one moment, it seems to fly around like a swarm of bees. The next, it's as scarce as martinis at a church service.

Mergers and acquisitions are inherently risky. When brands are in limbo, client relationships are as well. Competitors invariably seize opportunities to woo away both customers and employees—people who may already be pessimistic about the change.

If that's not enough to put everyone on edge—everyone knows you only have one chance to get it right! No pressure, right?

Through it all, if you keep your most important constituents in mind and adequately informed, they will continue to care about your brand. Or, perhaps, learn to care about the new one.

There are many positive actions you can take before, during and after a merger or acquisitions to numb the pain and keep as many stakeholders as possible in your camp.

Before the Merger

Costs

Mergers and acquisitions are not easy, nor are they inexpensive. Although in the long run, mergers and acquisitions create positive financial returns, in the beginning they take resources, sometimes pulling money and people away from operations.

To minimize this impact, it would be wise to build the rebrand into the cost of the deal. Doing so will require some deep diving into how much it will cost—but it's worth it. Most companies' marketing budgets don't have a lot of fat, so if they have to carry the weight of rebrands, something's got to give.

That something usually means lead generation activity, which you can't afford to cut back on during this volatile time. It's bad enough your marketing team will have to do double duty between the new brand launch and business as usual. Are you going to make them do it with their usual spend, as well? It won't work. Trust me.

Smart organizations do not choose between building a new brand and meeting monthly numbers. They are both important. Also, an expensive rebrand can make the cost of the deal less appealing. To know how much cost to build into the brand launch, every action needs to be planned out down to the smallest detail.

Naming

Before we consider the mechanics of a merger or acquisition, let's look at brand naming for the merged entity—an always complicated and usually frustrating task, since there are so many uncertainties involved.

This single aspect—the best name for a new entity forged from two distinct "others"—could easily become a book by itself. But for now, let's look at some of the major issues at play in the context of corporate branding in a time of merger or acquisition.

Should the name stay or should it go? As an acquiring company, this is a serious consideration. People care about the name—your employees, your customers, your community.

The "name should stay" choice

If you decide to stick with your existing brand going forward, you will need to spend more effort winning over the employees and customers associated with the disappearing brand. Remember, they probably don't have the same perception of your brand as you do. They probably don't care about the brand the way you do, either. And there's the real job: to make the transition one that promotes caring at every turn.

There are many justifiable reasons to keep your name on the door, including:

- Your company may enjoy significantly greater brand equity over the other.
- Rebranding costs may be more controllable as a function of the "stay" choice.
- A clearer connection to the acquired company's offerings may become more likely.
- Sometimes, the name on the check is the one that remains—just for simple vanity.

Listen without judgment to what others about the legacy brand. If there is a widespread perception about an untruth, don't fight it, just fix it as you plan the changeover. Don't waste time explaining why their misgivings are unfounded; simply agree that they exist, then demonstrate in positive terms why you've made the naming decisions you've settled upon. Remember, the goal is to get them to care, not for you to be right.

Think ahead about the messaging themes for the launch—and continually check with your various constituencies to ensure the themes are working as intended. Be flexible and listen to feedback from all quarters, all levels of involvement. Focus on why the brand matters. Make it a dialogue to ascertain what would make them care as much as you do.

And finally, act. Mean what you say, knowing that you must also *do* what you say. If you cannot do what people want, acknowledge it and explain the situation with as much transparency as you can. The only thing people hate more than not getting their way is believing they were never heard in the first place.

Remember, for this new iteration of the brand to succeed, you need people to care. That means: listening, messaging, and acting—proactively, sincerely and with commitment.

The "name should go" alternative

There are equally good reasons to start anew:

- It represents an opportunity for a fresh start to disengage from old perceptions and feelings attributable to the companies involved.
- There's an opening to make a bigger splash with a "brand new" company.
- It's a way to establish a more cohesive connection to the new company's combined offerings.
- It's a way to bring everyone involved together under a brand that's new to everyone, not just to some.

As with keeping the legacy name, proactivity, sincerity, and commitment to listening, messaging and actions are still vital, but with a much different focus.

The listening you'll do in the planning stages will be less about understanding what people recall about the past and more about what they perceive for the future of this new brand. This is your opportunity to team build. By engaging everyone in the conversation about the future and its opportunities, they will learn to care about the new brand because it's the one they feel they are helping to shape.

Throughout the process, it's important to message all of your constituent communities regularly, offering encouragement, recognition, and opportunity wherever you can. Remind them that with the new brand, there's an opportunity to bring a solution to all these new people.

Creating a new identity

At the risk of oversimplifying a very complex topic, here are some considerations to think about as you create a new name for a brand that's resulted from a merger/acquisition:

- **Get professional help.** The process will go much faster working with people who have done this before, and you'll run far less risk of having it to do over again. I once worked with a product that had three different names in five years because the internal people who named it thought they knew what they were doing.

- **Remember who you're naming the brand for.** It's not for the owners or for shareholders or for line management. You're naming it for its true owners—the customers, employees, suppliers and end users. Your new brand can also have a considerable impact on talent management. It's easier to attract top talent to an aptly named brand. Easier to keep them, too.

- **Check for opportunities to mock.** Be brutal on your brand name; your detractors will. When USAir changed its name to USAirways, it quickly became known as "US-scare-ways." While it's almost impossible to prevent all name hacking, try to make it difficult for people.

A Note for Either Scenario

Stay monogamous. When a new brand is on the scene, do not let the old ones stick around without prompt and direct reference to the new one, such as "Cogswell Cogs, now part of Spacely Sprockets." Yes, people may have business cards and there are old signs on display—but it's time to let go of the business cards and everything else associated with the old brand.

Build consensus among leadership

During mergers and acquisitions. the people at the helm of your organization must lead both employees and your customers through the uncharted waters of this new deal. One way to help assure cooperation is to provide for equal representation from both companies in senior positions. This sends the message that everyone is equal.

"Straight out the gate, when our CEO announced the leadership team, it was 50/50 Yahoo and AOL," Oath's Chief Marketing Officer Allie Kline told Marketing Week In 2017.[24] "That set the tone quickly by strongly indicating that we're not going to be more of one than the other. Culturally, it's about everybody sitting at the top table together."

"Tone" also comes into play across the board in times of great organizational change. It's crucial that leadership from both parties lands on the same page about the brand strategy and offers concrete expectations to guide all employees to implement it.

So before the deal is done, determine who can help unify the companies around a central brand. Recruit them for conspicuous roles of authority. It doesn't stop there. Make certain that they understand the brand strategy as it emerges, as well as just how it will make the merger go more smoothly, save money in the long run, highlight differentiation and drive business growth.

Many people in your new organization may not understand the concept of branding. It's crucial that everyone is on the same page. That's where merger-specific leadership comes in. Your senior and most influential people need to lead the troops through the process. So find "influencers" and be sure they fully understand both the principles and the operating details of their roles with regard to the strategy as a whole.

Work across the organization and its silos to find those who are already on the brand bandwagon. They're the ones who inherently understand the opportunity and are exceedingly positive about it. Then move on to influential colleagues who can help ensure the migration is taken seriously from the very beginning. Your senior people must be behind the work, or you will face a painful number of unnecessary push-backs.

The voids

A carefully planned, implemented and tweaked messaging strategy is the most important tool you have with regard to getting people to care about your new brand during mergers and acquisitions. And the key to messaging strategy is knowing where there are "voids."

Voids are any situations in which there is an unknown: an unanswered question, an unaddressed concern, an uncertain future.

Humans are exceedingly uncomfortable with voids. Know they are going to happen if you do not plan carefully for them. Some may pop up even if you do plan for them—so you'll need to be ready for those, too.

Employees

The first question on everyone's mind when a merger/acquisition is announced is: "Will I still have a job?"

During the largest merger and acquisition I have ever personally experienced, I would often engage with people in similar roles to mine from the acquired company. Some had far more experience than I, some less, some about the same. For almost everyone, the conversations were surreal, out of the blue and almost always uncomfortable. I remember asking myself, "Why is he telling me this?" when a future colleague was discussing the challenges of his job, most which came from his boss. Then it dawned on me: "They think I'm going to be their new boss!" Of course, I was thinking the same about many of them!

People did not know what was happening, so they filled in one void by making assumptions about their new manager.

Most of these situations arise from lack of reliable information and are filled with fear, which leads to extreme thinking like: "everyone is getting laid off," "they're shipping all the jobs to India," or "none of the acquired company's managers will get good roles." Because they have no other credible information, others then come to believe the rumors. The next thing you know, morale slows productivity to a standstill, good talent walks out the door, and time that should have been devoted to earning the honest and open care of employees and customers alike is spent doing damage control.

That's the information void. What about the emotional void?

Many companies invest a great deal of time and money creating positive and inclusive workplace environments. As we've discussed, we want to give employees the chance to take pride in their work, to identify with it, to make it an integral part of their lives. The focal point of that emotional investment is, of course, the brand.

What happens when you take it away? Right, it leaves a void. People who spend the bulk of their waking hours at work will naturally feel a bit lost and empty when the familiar and comfortable setting is quite suddenly taken away. They will feel somehow damaged and hurt, as well.

Then there's the physical void.

In so many cases, those who survive a layoff will continue to work alongside empty desks. If you've never had to do that, I can tell you that working in this type of environment is depressing and toxic. It doesn't matter that those desks may have been home to your break room nemesis or your work wife. The departure of your colleagues is hard to take.

Physical voids can also impose disturbing factors such as new company locations that require altered commutes, new offices that just don't feel right and new people as office mates.

Most people are uncomfortable, at least at some level, with change of any kind. Nowhere is this more evident than when one's environment changes. Long-term employees have often built their entire lives around their work addresses. A new location on the other side of the city might add hours to their commutes. And for some, moving homes, families and community involvement is just not worth it.

Of course, you can't avoid many of these realities. However, if you discuss these changes, you can help keep these voids from happening and enjoy a lot more success. In other words, listen to those affected, assist in whatever ways you can, and make it as easy as possible for those who need help with the inevitable adjustments brought on by major change.

Celebrate More

Another way to maintain migration momentum is to schedule regular updates with clients, employees and other stakeholders. Have a plan in place to highlight migration wins at 30, 90, 120 days, and so forth. It's even more important to celebrate your "brand champions" from the start, particularly the more influential ones.

Educate

Before you launch the new brand, have a brand education program ready. Some people may do whatever they're told without understanding why. Few will do it well. When people know why the brand is important, when they understand how their support of it will lead to the organization's success, they are far more likely to work with its best interests at heart. And they will leave behind their old brand allegiance for the new much one more quickly.

One element of a brand education program that is especially relevant to mergers or acquisitions is the role of brand ambassador. Brand ambassadors are people within in your organization who, like brand champions, are excited by the prospects of the new brand. However, brand ambassadors are representatives whom you've trained to help your colleagues navigate through some of the simpler elements of the brand. They are cheerleaders, role models—great sources of positive energy during times when it is most needed.

Governance

It's important to remember that a governance program—the law and order of who can make which decisions about what in a variety of situations—is crucial to a brand's healthy development and well-being. Think through as much as you can before the party starts, so to speak, but make it clear that rules may change as the brand evolves.

Customers, before the merger

Customers will surely questions have questions as well about how the change will affect them:

- Will prices increase?
- Will the level and quality of the services I get stay the same, improve or devolve?

- Will my account person change?

And that final question brings up an often-hidden item—personal relationships. Frequently a client, customer or vendor will have worked closely with one of your employees over time, and personal relationships may have emerged. Taking away that "comfort level" can create anxiety.

But what if the anxiety gives your brand's competitors the chance to tell their story? Rumors abound about management shake-ups, stalled products, mass exoduses—the soap opera script practically writes itself. Be certain to put forth a narrative from the start that would supplant any theorizing from the competition. Remember, once something is said, it's true if people want to believe it. Make certain your story is the one they choose to believe.

Much like your company's veteran employees and long-term customers, it's crucial to make your new arrivals feel welcome in this new corporate environment. Show special interest in them. Find out what they liked most about working with the company you've just acquired—and what they didn't. Outline the new roadmap and how you plan to be with them for the long haul.

Earning customer goodwill that results in caring during mergers and acquisitions requires four key elements:

- Listening
- Repeating back
- Demonstrating
- Reassuring

Make certain that the most important and profit-generating clients have the ear of someone at your company with enough gravitas to do something about their concerns. Otherwise, don't waste their time.

Repeat back what they told you, both on the spot and after the fact. And pass this information along to their account people so they, too, will understand the concerns.

Find tangible ways to demonstrate that you have heard them and taken their points of view seriously.

Finally, reassure them any way that makes sense. For example, regular correspondence from the CEO about the transition can go a long way, assuming it's genuine, honest and future-focused.

Anticipating the competition's response

You're almost done preparing for the merger. But don't forget your competitors. Sit down with your trusted colleagues and brainstorm. Come up with anything mean, nasty, unattractive or unkind that the competition might say about your new brand—valid or not. Then, from these discussions and well in advance of any merger announcement, develop as much responsive and proactive content as possible to pre-empt any of those nasty rumors before they start.

During the Merger

What will make employees care during the transition period? We know voids are bad, but what about in the heat of the transition?

First, celebrate their past. You want the people who are joining your company to care about your brand—even while they still care about the brand you just purchased. Don't make them feel bad for caring about what they think they've lost. Help them celebrate what they've accomplished with their previous brand and promise them they will have to opportunity to have even grander pride as part of the new brand.

There's a fine line to be drawn here—a balancing act between celebrating the past and keeping it there. If you saw the movie "Jobs," there was that great scene in which Steve Wozniak tried to get Steve Jobs to recognize how the contributions of the Apple II team helped the company's launch of the Macintosh. Jobs refused again and again. On this point, Jobs was in the wrong and Woz was right. It costs nothing to recognize the work of others. In fact, this step is particularly important when referencing work from a minority party of the business.

For example: If, in a post-acquisition speech or letter to the new company as a whole, the CEO harkens back to the day of its earliest products, he or she should also reference the older products, key policies and pivotal people throughout the history of the acquired company. After all, those successes added the very value that made the firm worthy of being acquired. Not only does this praise and recognition come for free in dollar terms, it's not done at anyone's reputational expense.

Let's always remember that there's an infinite amount of goodwill to go around before, during and after a merger. Spread that goodwill liberally if you want to create a culture in which mergers and acquisitions go well, meet all their goals, and grow both the brand and its business.

Cross lead

Do everything you can to blur the line between the acquiring and the acquired company—to avoid the caustic comment, "Are you Legacy United or Legacy Continental?" Every time that distinction is made adds days, weeks or months to the timeline for true integration.

One easy way to blur the line is have a Company A leader talk about an advancement made by a Company B team, and vice versa. Doing this suggests that management no longer thinks of A and B...so why should we?

Use analogies. Say a long-time, almost iconic employee retires. He has been a mentor to more people than he can count. Throughout his career, he has led the company through lots of wins, birthed many new ideas and helped nearly everyone grow. Yet, it is time and he is leaving.

Even though he will no longer show up to work each day, people still carry with them the lessons he taught. Give employees the opportunity to give thanks for having known him, but don't let them call him back out of retirement every time there is a new challenge. Instead, give them the opportunity to get to know the new guy. Give them time. Give them space.

Give them something to look forward to

If you don't give them something new to focus on they will still work as if the old brand has not yet left the building. Alternatively, they could just follow their own path, which would be a shame with so much institutional knowledge walking out the door into the arms of your competitors. So set milestones, talk up their importance and give everyone something to celebrate once they happen. Make it clear that meeting those milestones matters.

Someone purchased the brand or orchestrated this merger for a reason. Without jeopardizing proprietary information, ensure that everyone understands the direction your brand will be taking, why that's the best route, what will be required, and what their role will be along the way. Just as important, make sure each individual understands that everyone else on the team needs them and their contributions.

They will not care if they do not understand why the journey matters—and why they matter to the journey.

CHAPTER 5: WHO ELSE CARES?

Employees make it happen and customers pay the bills—so why does it matter if everyone else cares?

True, employees and customers are your most important priorities but every team needs a cheering section. Yours is made up of the media, Wall Street analysts, industry experts and even elected officials.

Does the News Media?

In 2016, the global PR industry was worth an estimated $14 billion. If this doesn't seem like an astronomical sum, consider what it means: $14 billion being spent on phrasing blurbs in just the right ways, writing statements for PR Newswire and shining a positive spotlight on negative company news. To put it bluntly, companies are spending billions on spin.

CEOs themselves are also getting in on the act. A growing number of them are looking for that certain sound bite that stands out in an interview, something that will make them the darling of the business press. Michael O'Leary, CEO of Europe's biggest airline, Ryanair, is notorious for generating quotable sound bites. Hundreds of articles have been devoted to his controversial statements. Is it effective? Well, ask yourself this: Who knows the name of Lufthansa's CEO?

Getting the media to care about your brand is a must. It will make everything you do grow your brand and your business more quickly and effectively. Being a familiar figure in the media gives you credibility with reporters and editors, even if what they're saying isn't always completely flattering. The simple fact that the media takes time to cover you sends a message to readers (and other reporters) that you're relevant. You are, at least, worth a second look.

To capture and sustain the media's attention, it's important to understand what's important to them. Here are some thoughts to consider.

Nobody's patsy

The last thing you want to do is make someone from the media think that they are simply a conduit for getting your information out there. Treat your media interactions like a partnership, remembering that they owe you nothing. In fact, it's usually the other way around. You need them far more than they need you, especially in the beginning.

This dynamic also means that you shouldn't expect them to write only good things about the company or the brand. Your main goal is to come out after each interaction looking good overall. Reporters and editors are unlikely to make something up. They're also unlikely to be intentionally unfair. In fact, exposing a few warts every now and then may actually give your brand a certain balance, a perceived credibility. Do you want people to see you as too good to be true? For most brands these days, too good to be true is a red flag, while imperfection is okay.

If you're an advertiser with a media outlet, do not assume that the dollars you are investing in ads entitle your brand to any favorable coverage in that medium. Most legitimate news organizations have an iron curtain between the advertising department and the editorial desk.

(This phenomenon may not apply to some trade publications, but it's always best to assume it does.) So please don't insult reporters or interviewers by suggesting that they work for you, given that your advertising dollars pay their salary. Trust me, that will not end well.

Before trying to win over any media, be certain you understand what is important to each of them.

Keep in mind that when you're in the throes of promoting your work, it's easy to forget that others are nowhere near as passionate about your work as you are. Just because it's important to you doesn't make important to them. No one else cares. That's why you have to approach each of your media contacts in ways that help them in their work.

Like you, media outlets have competitors and are always looking for content that is relevant and competitively differentiated from others in their space. They want to provide the best content and focus on topics that will interest and inform as many of their readers or listeners as possible. So, don't try to get *Car & Driver* to write about your new meal service. Likewise, *WIRED* won't care about your aftermarket automobile accessories.

Make yourself available—whenever

Relationships with journalists should not be one-night stands. Think of them more as long-term friends with benefits: you're not going to marry them exclusively, but you'll always want to have the option for a fling—and they should feel the same way. You should make yourself available to them whenever they need you. If you can't personally help them when they need you, find someone on your team who can. As always, approach the necessary function of media relations as just that—a relationship.

Promote them back

When their coverage of your work is mostly positive, promote it. Make certain your social channels recognize the work, the outlet and the writer by name. It's an easy way for you to give them credit and for you to promote yourself at the same time.

Be as transparent as possible

When working with a reporter, it's always important to be as transparent and authentic as you can be, given any corporate or brand constraints. For example, if you have to change the time of an interview, a media person will be more likely to work with you if he or she knows why the schedule needs to change.

London-based entertainment reporter James Body shared with me this anecdote: "I was recently covering a brand and they had to reschedule the interview, but they did not sugarcoat the reason why. They got straight to the point. Without that kind of transparency, many reporters would not want to accommodate the request. But because they were so transparent, I was happy to reschedule the interview. I'd also hope that someday, if the tables are turned and I need some flexibility, that I will be forthcoming, as well, and receive their flexibility in return."

Authenticity matters

Body recommends brands not to be afraid the be straight with the media. "There's a sense out there that you have to be perfect and polished. It's okay if you come across a little rough and ready. It's actually more believable. A little bit of the human side can go a long way. Plus, things have changed now. It used to be that if it were in print, it was the truth. Now, information is a lot more subjective, so…the more authentic you are, the more believable you will be."

Take the high road

If something goes wrong—if you get a bad review or there is a massive misunderstanding that leads to bad coverage—do what you can to control damage but take the high road. Instead of calling the writer "incompetent" or "unfair" in public, lament that you did not clear up the misunderstanding before it was too late. Profess respect for the individual yet disagree strongly if you must.

Does the Government Care?

Customers care about the wheeling and dealing of companies, even if it's tempting to believe that two huge firms merging is the sole concern of Wall Street analysts and the financial press. A good example was seen with the proposed 2014 acquisition of Time Warner by telecom giant Comcast. What could be more infuriating to consumers than the possibility of two notoriously unpopular companies joining forces?

When Comcast CEO Bryan L Roberts tried to make the $45 billion deal happen, customers across the United States made sure their disapproval was heard. Over 400,000 people signed a petition urging the Department of Justice to block the deal from going through. One head of a popular consumer action group said at the time, "Consumers are fed up with Comcast and Time Warner Cable, which already rank toward the bottom when it comes to customer satisfaction."[25]

In addition to the public outcry, more than 50 consumer advocacy groups across the country lent their voices to the protest. The government listened to the uproar. Eventually, in early 2015, Comcast abandoned the acquisition altogether amid objections from the Federal Communications Commission, the Department of Justice—and most probably because consumers let them know in no uncertain terms that they wouldn't back the new company.

A McKinsey survey found that the potential variance in business value at stake from government intervention and regulation is between 30% and 50% in most industries. The survey also found that fewer than 30% of executives believed their external affairs groups had the organizational structure in place to succeed in their ventures.[26]

Why can't companies establish a comfort level relative to what they deem to be an effective set of government relations policies? Failure to match the parameters of the policy with governmental criteria is frequently mentioned, as is skepticism about what such policies would achieve if they were in place. But most prevalent is the doubt that the people responsible for government relations are the best-suited company contacts with government at all levels.

When the value at stake is so significant, it seems unwise not to at least look at how your firm could achieve this. It would involve at least some of the following elements.

- **Identify a government affairs contact in your organization.** The government—be it city, state or federal—needs to have a direct line to one designated person in your organization. Ideally, the individual will be a consensus-builder who can align thinking inside your organization as well as outside.

- **Develop a support committee.** The government affairs contact shouldn't operate in a vacuum. He or she should be able to relay progress at dedicated intervals—say, once a month—to an internal committee that can help formulate plans of action and carry feedback to and from their own departments.

- **Establish goals/write a mission statement.** What does the company want to achieve from government relations? As with all businesses, it's useful to have a mission statement from the outset. This statement should be clear, easy to understand, and the driving force of all communications with government.

- **Identify relevant offices of government.** The next step is to identify which state or federal departments are most likely to help your organization achieve its goals. Identify the legislator personally, if possible, and arrange an introductory meeting at which you transmit in clear, plain language what you want to achieve in the mid- and long-term.

- **Begin networking.** This is arguably the most important item on the list. It's why you appoint a consensus-builder to the role of government liaison officer. Ideally, this would involve offering an industry-level sounding board to government officials.

- **Invite legislators to events.** When organizing conferences, banquets or other events, make an effort to include government officials on the list of invitees—or as speakers. Very often, they will welcome the opportunity to raise their own profile, giving you yet another opportunity to build links.

- **Maintain regular communication.** At this point, your organization will have a better feel for how to interact with government and how those interactions could be improved. Keep regular contact, and maintain awareness of government programs, grants, and events that would be beneficial to your organization.

- **Be transparent.** When interacting with government officials, it's best to be transparent at all times. Wherever possible, keep a log of meetings and other communications. This will also help drive the agenda at your internal committee meetings.

Does the Public Care?

There are many brands that have trouble hiring good talent because of the public perception issues. Even potential employees pay close attention to the branding of their suitors.

According to analysis by online job aggregator Betterteam, companies with brands that are perceived positively attract twice as many applicants as comparable firms with branding that is viewed in a less positive light. Missing out on attracting top talent may generate significant costs further down the chain.[27]

A study by the Harvard Business Review and ICM Unlimited found that companies with a negative reputation could spend over 10% more per hire. Naturally, as firms get larger, these costs stack up. And that's if you can even manage to attract the talent—in many cases, they won't come on board in the first place, even with a higher salary. This highlights the importance of ensuring branding is effective enough to attract applicants.[28]

Sometimes your customers care but don't necessarily realize it—so you have to remind them how much they care.

For example, I am personally not a big fan of parades. This dates back to my college days of living in a fraternity house directly on a parade route that featured marching bands seemingly every Saturday morning. Marching bands. Saturday mornings. College. Those three things do not mesh.

Recently, however, I had the opportunity to march in a parade, and my perspective changed significantly. The setting was the annual Carnival Parade in Provincetown, Massachusetts. Following the 2016 Pulse nightclub massacre in Orlando, Florida, my friend, who manages events for JetBlue, made the case for the brand to support the town's large LGBT community by having a presence in the parade. Throughout the two-mile parade route, we handed out small gifts such as cardboard fans, mints, and keychains. We also handed out several round-trip tickets—unbeknownst to the crowd except for the lucky few who received them.

The response was eye-opening: screams of "We love JetBlue!" and "Yay, JetBlue!" were heard along the parade route, along with comments such as "JetBlue's the best" and "They're the only decent airline left."

Be present

We get to know each other as people by spending time with one another—by being present in each others' lives. It's the same with brands. If you want the world to care about your brand, be present. Be present in your community, your industry, and in the areas that matter to you and your customers.

Being present in your community can take many forms, of course, especially when almost all we do is virtual these days. Sponsoring a local children's football team is a good start. By being present, you become less of a "they" and more of a "we."

A 2016 Nielsen study found that the majority of corporate leaders (61%) identified "doing what's right" as the reason behind their corporate responsibility efforts. However, only 41% of the general public thought that was their motives, while 43% assumed it was for publicity.[29]

In this age of cynicism, we should not find these numbers surprising, but they do provide a nice reminder to consider our motivations and intent carefully. The primary driver behind any corporate presence in the community should not be to engender its care.

Seems a bit duplicitous to you, does it? Why bring it up at all in this book then? Here's an analogy. Maintaining a healthy weight and staying active is the right thing to do because it puts less strain on our organs and can prolong our lifespans. Yes, people might like the way we look because of it, too, but is that correct the primary driver?

The key is authenticity in meaning and message. As Nielsen's Chris McAllister writes in Uncommon Sense: Are companies totally committed to social responsibility?":

"Authenticity in communications is also important. Today, virtually everyone believes companies should communicate their CSR efforts. But approximately half of those surveyed feel that the way companies do it is too self-serving. Not surprisingly, consumers respond better to a low-key, informational approach, such as reporting CSR activities on a website or in an annual report sought out by already-interested consumers, than to anything with an obvious promotional element."[30]

Talent Plus, a talent assessment agency in Lincoln, Nebraska, involves its own employees in their community presence. Kimberly

Shirk, who, in addition to her day job as Senior Marketing Strategist, also serves as Corporate Responsibility Chair, explains that the company uses pillars, or key focus areas, to evaluate on community outreach.

"Corporate Social Responsibility for us is a deeply held belief aimed directly at impacting the surrounding community in significant ways," Shirk says. "For us, that extends internationally, as well. Each year, we survey our associates and ask them, along with our leadership team, for their input in choosing what we call Social Responsibility Pillars. Our employees choose four pillars each year, based on the following criteria:

- Talent Plus, in partnering with the leadership of the organizations, can achieve the greatest impact by aligning with each client's organization.
- Collectively cover local, national and international regions to allow associates in our extended community to participate fully.

Talent Plus employees contribute their time and talent toward aligning with each pillar's mission for the year.

"It's important to us for a couple of strong reasons," Shirk continues, "because each associate votes on what our focus will be for the year, and because we are a human resource consulting company, we know the powerfully positive effect that talented, passionate individuals can have on the community at large.

"It benefits our brand because when our associates are in the community, the community members see the power of having a highly talented team working with each non-profit." She also says, "It's a great source of engagement, and we know that engagement increases the likelihood of retention, productivity and ultimately profitability.

"I would hate to witness what would happen if it did not exist," she says. "This past year, as we applied for the Great Place To Work award, the social responsibility program got a 100% approval rating for the question: "I feel good about the ways we contribute to the community.

"It's a sense of pride around here, not just for the Leadership team, but the entire company. Our corporate social responsibility is woven into the core of who we are."

CHAPTER 6: DO YOU CARE TO CHANGE?

Every company needs to continually look at its brands and how they are perceived to ensure that its customers and employees still care.

Much of the work we perform is consulting with companies whose brands have languished over the years, or with organizations that have not developed a cohesive brand strategy at all—or perhaps haven't paid enough attention to the one they've been living with all these years.

The right brand strategy can make an enormous difference in each of these hypothetical situations, which is why it's crucial to measure and evaluate how much a company's constituencies care. Here are five reasons to consider:

- Brand strategies align an organization. They help ensure that all areas of the business are working toward the same goals of fulfilling the brand promise and holistically building relationships with customers.

- Your brand strategy should drive how you bring new offerings to the market. It can help you focus on exactly what will make you relevant and competitively differentiated from the other options your customers may have.

- Marketing is hard in the best of scenarios. If your message and creative is disjointed, the offers and the hooks have to work harder than usual, often alienating potential customers rather than attracting them.

- A brand strategy provides context for bringing the brand to life. When the brand's personality attributes are well articulated and tightly aligned with everything else about the brand, the creative process is invigorated.

- People work for more than a paycheck. The strongest brand strategies inspire and engage employees, both new hires and long-time associates.

How many of these areas represent "one-and-done" kinds of functions? None. That is why is essential to look at our brand strategies for signs they need to evolve or change.

We work hard to impress upon our clients that when they adopt a brand strategy, commitment to executing it is necessary—but that doesn't mean forever. As the world evolves and your customers' needs change, so should your brand strategy—as long as you do it thoughtfully, judiciously, authentically and in a way that will not confuse your customers or employees. All of which leads inevitably to this question: "How will I know when to re-evaluate my brand strategy?"

Well, that depends. We live in a data-driven world in which the perceptions, emotions, and sentiments associated with a particular brand can change rapidly and radically, sometimes in what seems like just the blink of an eye. That's why so many organizations invest in brand-related research activities.

In fact, most organizations surveyed in a 2017 Spencer Brenneman study—97.3%—reported that they commit at least some resources directly to brand research. For half of them, brand-related research is a continual activity and is part of their standard operating procedures.

For another 40%, it's conducted twice per year. And the remaining 10% execute some research activities annually. All of the respondents allocate at least some resources to brand research.[31]

What activities do they emphasize? Customer/client surveys are the most common brand research method (35.6%), only slightly more popular than market research (32.9%). Other methods include social media analytics (11.6%), focus groups (10.6%) and SEO analytics (8.2%).

The major conclusion of our study was that research pays off. A clear majority of respondents reported increasing their brand strategy investment over the past five years, while an almost equal number reported continually researching on the brand.

Another way research can pay off is in preventing unwarranted rebranding campaigns in the first place. If an organization is constantly managing its brand, they will know when it's time for a tweak. When potentially negative trends begin to appear, ongoing research will help to ensure that they don't pile up and the company can quickly respond.

Is Change Possible?

Brand strategy shifts usually happen as part of a broader operational change. In fact, a strategy shift is often the way the brand signals to the customer that "things are changing around here." When implemented properly, effective brand strategy shifts can create enormous value.

Examples abound. When McDonald's reputation took a hit in the early part of the last decade—in no small part because of the 2001 book Fast Food Nation and the "Super Size Me" documentary (2004)—management decided its brand needed an overhaul. In response, they began moving the company away from being a "fast food cafe" and toward being a "restaurant."[32]

This overhaul came to life in a number of ways, such as eliminating its uncomfortable plastic furniture. Gone, too, was the small one-size-fits-all menu, replaced by gourmet "signature craft burgers." Today's McDonald's looks nothing like it did a generation ago.

Similarly, Xerox's management decided a shift in brand strategy was overdue. Despite having significantly diversified into a broad spectrum of back-office services, Xerox was still strongly identified with copiers, an area that didn't hold many growth prospects now that most documents were exchanged digitally.

In 2008, the company began a rebrand that changed the corporate logo, removing the emphasis it had placed on its roots as a copier firm.[33] John Kennedy, Xerox CMO, said of the shift, "Despite already being recognized as a leading global brand, there was a gap between our brand perception versus our brand reality—particularly on the services side."[34]

Avoid the Word "Paradigm"

Our world continually changes, sometimes slowly, sometimes quickly. The roles women play in society, for instance, have slowly evolved over the years (more slowly than they should have, of course, but that's another topic). These slow shifts have often affected how companies market, the products and services they offer, and the consumers to whom they market. Conversely, the smartphone quickly changed how we interact with one another, consume content, even shop. Let's take a look at what all this can mean to you.

According to personnel consulting firms FlexJobs and Brie Weiler Reynolds, 58% of the U.S. workforce will be freelancing by 2027. That means fewer people to fight other commuters or wage war on roads and in airports. However, this radical change will also mean that fewer people will build personal work relationships, experience random acts of kindness, shake hands, experience hugs or share lunch with someone else on any given day. Most importantly, this sea change means that it will be more and more difficult for us all to meet our basic human need for connection.

As this trend continues, critical judgments will need to be exercised by thousands of companies regarding how their brand strategy can reconnect them with their clients.

One leading-edge technology employer is already creating differentiation. With more than 800 employees worldwide, Carbon Black has a distributed workforce, like most technology firms. Nonetheless, regardless of role or rank, every new hire is flown to the company's Waltham, Massachusetts, headquarters within the first 90 days (and within the first 30 for senior executives).

"The program is called Team First," explains Amy Robinson, Chief People Officer, Carbon Black. "It's important that all our employees develop connections across geographical borders and throughout the organization. All of the training modules they experience during their visit are presented by senior executives."

I suspect that we will see more of this nurturing as the months and years go by. Start planning now.

Technology

In 2008, I was involved in the creation of the multi-million dollar launch of a new, global brand—a visual identity system. The concept caught on and was working well for two years—and then, along came the iPad.

It hadn't been on anyone's radar, but suddenly our almost brand new visual identity system was out of date. Our color scheme had been created for a predominately print-based system, and our web guidelines did not easily translate to the interactivity of these new devices. Even the imaginative logo we designed did not fit naturally into the available space on these devices. Technology had caused an unexpected, earthquake-like shift.

Money

When I was a child, layaway was a thing. Credit cards were not yet popular, and their interest rates were prohibitive for most people.

However, by the time I headed to college, there was easier access to credit, and interest rates had plunged. Banking technology evolved, too, so more vendors were able to sell items without the cumbersome warehousing requirements of layaway. Brands that were perceived as layaway companies now had competition from others who could just hand over merchandise at the swipe of a card.

What is changing for your business with regard to money? "Cryptocurrencies" are becoming more popular every day. While I have no specific point of view on the topic, I can see how the potential of a cryptocurrency is enough to give many brands a valid reason to look and listen for possible reasons to change some elements of their brand strategies.

It should come as no surprise that the first auto manufacturer to accept bitcoin was Tesla. Why on earth would the brand known for successfully breaking all the rules follow the mundane constraints of archaic, gold-backed currencies? Going crypto is totally on-brand for Tesla. Would we view Ford any differently if it had been the first? Other retailers, like Overstock.com, are on board, as is online dating service OKCupid. If the cryptocurrency phenomenon takes off, as many think it will, then what does the early association of these diverse firms say about their brands? And what does it say about their competitors?

Mores

Massachusetts, where I live and work, is known for a large number of arcane "blue laws" in its legal system, conventions that have persisted over many decades. For instance, retailers may open at any time on Sunday without the need for approval by the Department of Labor Standards and without the need for a local police permit—except for retailers of alcoholic beverages! These stores may not open until 10 a.m. on Sunday. But this wasn't always the case.

Once, not too long ago, retailers were not allowed to sell any alcoholic beverages at all on Sundays. But over time, as society became less and less religious, more and more secular, these laws faced increased scrutiny. Another reason for change, of course, was that people living in the communities on the border of other states that didn't have such restrictive laws simply crossed state lines. Great for non-Massachusetts retailers—but only until the blue laws changed. Nowadays, everyone should be on the lookout for changing moral and behavioral codes and how such changes might one day impact their businesses and their brands.

What mores are changing for you? Certainly, as marriage equality for same-sex couples becomes a reality around the world, employer brands must keep up with new lifestyle choices. Beyond that, retailers and some service businesses may find new opportunities for accommodating transgender individuals.

Brands are also increasingly eager to reach out to the lesbian, gay, bisexual, transgender (LGBT) community, even if it might risk offending the more conservative segments of society. Chevrolet's 2013 campaign ads—under the heading "Find New Roads"—broke new ground by including a vignette featuring a gay couple.[35] What's more, when faced with criticism for that approach, the company stood its ground and was totally unapologetic with respect to including the couple.

In 2013, Cheerios featured an interracial couple and their daughter, generating so many racist comments on YouTube that the section had to be closed. However, the video's likes outnumbered the dislikes two to one.[36]

The ad had received more than 1,600 likes and more than 500 dislikes as of Thursday evening.

Despite the hate, Camille Gibson, vice president of marketing for Cheerios, told us in a statement, "Consumers have responded positively to our new Cheerios ad. At Cheerios, we know there are many kinds of families and we celebrate them all."[37]

Appealing to the fringe elements of society is important to brands, and not just because it includes profitable niche markets. Differences based on ethnicity, color, gender and sexuality are all regularly referenced by brands as they seek to appeal to everyone by showing that everyone does, indeed, mean everyone.

For example, in 2013, Guinness aired its "Friendship" commercial for the first time. It featured six men playing wheelchair basketball and revealed, at the end of the ad, that only one of the men was truly physically disabled. Although less than 1% of Americans depend on wheelchairs for mobility, the commercial had universal appeal.

Changing gender roles

While the employment section of the U.S. Civil Rights Act of 1964 prohibited discrimination on the grounds of gender, more than 50 years later, women are still considerably behind their male counterparts in terms of workplace status. In 2017, for example, only 32 Fortune 500 companies had female CEOs, representing a 6% of the total.[38]

This is remarkable, not only because of the blatant sexism inherent in the statistic but also because it is now widely accepted that women drive the majority of consumer purchases. By some estimates, over 70% of consumer purchases are decided by women.[39]

Brands have finally awakened to the reality. Look at commercials for washing machines from the 1950s, in which depictions of a woman happily filling a washing machine with the family clothes were ubiquitous. Today, the same companies know that marketing in this way would be suicide.

Elsewhere, since beginning its "Real Beauty" campaign in 2004, Dove products have gained a whole new range of female customers, who "want to be communicated with in totality—not just as some little girl's 'mom' or some man's helpmate."[40]

Artificial intelligence (AI)

Artificial intelligence will propel enormous changes—in practically every brand. Soon, our refrigerators will order more milk for us when we're running out. Our table lamps will tell us when the school bus is near. One pill will tell our doctor how well other pills are working.

For gadget addicts and brand geeks alike, this news is really exciting. Experts forecast the eventual size of the "Internet of Things" market could grow to $19 trillion a year. The gadget addict in me gets excited just thinking about how technology is already connecting our lives in ways that were unimaginable just a few short years ago. Apple Carplay? Love it! Alexa calls the shots at my house. And we are just getting started.

On a more practical level, the brand strategist in me sees an enormous opportunity here to differentiate your brands by finding creative ways to use artificial intelligence to connect with customers in more meaningful ways.

What might that look like? We could spend weeks and weeks hypothesizing about AI's potential and still barely scratch the surface. For your employer brand? Perhaps virtual assistants to order lunch when an employee's calendar leaves no time for a break. Or perhaps the calendar automatically schedules a lunch break (in real time) after a series of back-to-back meetings and orders an individualized menu for each attendee.

For B2B and B2C customers

Granted, we have leveraged triggered campaigns for years. However, the idea of sending an email reminding an automobile owner that it's time for an oil change will become roughly equivalent to the Wright Brothers' first contraption when compared to the Boeing Dreamliner and Airbus A380s of today.

Alexa for business is not only creating personal assistants in the workplace—as well as low-level desktop support—but Amazon now offers application programming interfaces (APIs) created just for businesses. For example, if you sell any kind of research, a customized Alexa skill could create considerable differentiation for you, for example: "Alexa, ask Acme Research how many people will work remotely in 2027."

In fact, IBM Watson is already on track to create considerable AI differentiation for many big brands.

For example, Christina Mercer, reporting in the July 2017 issue of Computerworld UK, notes that Condé Nast has partnered with a company called "Influence" to use IBM's Watson to better target prospects for social media campaigns.

"The software built by IBM and Influential, (a 'data-first influencer platform') offers Condé Nast customers (such as the *New Yorker* and *Vogue*) insight into who should be prime targets for their sales effort, and which celebrities would make the best brand ambassadors in each specific product situation," reports Mercer.

But how would this happen? Watson reviews huge amounts of data (including emojis) to identify and qualify influencers who are compassionate or authoritative. So be careful how you use those eggplant and martini-glass emojis!

The moral of this story is: Pay attention and always look for overt and subtle changes that can impact your business and perhaps alter the effectiveness of your branding strategies. Sometimes you won't be aware of a shift until a major change has already occurred.

Telltale signs

In addition to continual research and extensive paradigm shifts, there are other tell-tale signs that your brand may need a refresh.

- **Sales is from Mars and service is from Venus.** Is there a disconnect between what customers expect and what they get once they are on board? Are your customer service colleagues incessantly calibrating customer expectations once the sales team hands them over?

- **Innovation degradation.** You have a new product. It's exciting! It's life-changing. It's…a flop. Once launched, it does nothing to inspire buyers or set you apart from the competition.
- **Your campaigns are wearing lead shoes.** Are the response rates to social media and content marketing slowing to a crawl? Are your inbound marketing efforts working harder and harder but showing weaker and weaker results?
- **It's Groundhog Day, every day.** Does your creative process seem to take longer and longer, and does each iteration seems to move further away from the end goal? Can the team even articulate the end goal?
- **Too many going away parties.** Are you finding it harder and harder to attract and retain the best talent? Perhaps your employees aren't "feeling it" any longer and are finding other brands that will engage them with more than a paycheck.

Coat of paint or bulldozer?

You've determined that change is afoot and it's time to do something about it. But what? How much? When? Updating your visual identity is a lot different from creating a new one that represents a completely different set of values and philosophies. So, which is it? Paintbrush or bulldozer?

The first way is to ask your customers where they see their business now and where they see it going. Look carefully and objectively at how you're meeting those needs now and will continue to do so in the future. This assignment is a tough one. Third-parties can help you do it right—the first time.

Important Warning

Too often companies think that because their leaders or star players have been in business for so many years, they know all they need to know about the market. They do not. Ever. No one knows their industry so well that they cannot learn something new from a second pair of eyes.

Here's a case in point: Someone once vented to me that a potential employee didn't show him enough reverence or desire for the job. "She's got to be doing everything she can to impress me in order to work here." The offended party had just opened an online startup. With no other full-time employees. Without funding. Without office space beyond his dining room table. He just had a good idea and the beginnings of some good code behind it. But in his mind, his startup was already a success. It was already the next big thing. It was already "Uber for blah, blah, or blah." That's great! That's the kind of passion, vision and commitment needed to make any organization successful.

The problem is the disconnect between what we feel on the inside and what others see and think. We must constantly remind ourselves—whether we are a startup or a storied multinational—that we live and breathe our work and our brand. Others do not. We take for granted that special knowledge and understanding of our dream and mission that is only communicated to the outside world by nuance, and patiently, over long periods of time.

What do you need to keep in mind when looking into that mirror? Here are five practical suggestions:

- Be clear from the start about what you want to learn. Do not expect to understand everything, especially in the beginning.
- Ask for the kinds of help that will allow you to discover what you don't know.
- Remember it's not all about you: Look at your competitors' brands, too.
- Think of research as an ongoing process or effort. It's not a one and done exercise.
- Align the research with specific key performance indicators (KPIs) that are important to you. If a certain demographic is key to expansion plans, research them in that context.

Don't confuse the present with the future. Understand who you are and, more importantly, seek to understand how others see you.

Remember to ask your employees not only where they see your customers' businesses going, but also where they see their careers and their lives going. If the number of organizational layers within your company makes it difficult for employees to see a clear career path, or if you're the last one in your industry to offer paternity leave, wouldn't you want to know about these items before the best and brightest walk out the door?

Sleuth

Don't forget your competitors. The whole point of a brand is to create an emotional connection with your customers that is uniquely relevant and competitively differentiated from the other options they have. Sleuth doesn't imply anything illegal or resembling espionage. But do your homework. Get a sense of how competitors are perceived relative to you. Pay attention to their social media chatter. Participate in industry associations where others may have gotten wind of their plans.

I would never suggest that you follow your competitors' leads or beat them to whatever they're doing. Nor do I think it's necessarily a good idea to do what they're doing. The goal is to be so unquestionably different from your competitors that there is no real choice for your audiences but your brand.

In the early days of the iPhone, Apple locked its brand differentiation into place by building an ecosystem that not only sold more products but married customers to its other products in the process. Take a photo on your phone? It's on your computer automatically. Change a contact telephone number on your computer? No need to do it on your phone. Want to send text messages to friends from your computer? If they're on an iPhone, have at it!

Create a blank canvas

Once you've done your due diligence, try this experiment: Knowing what you know now, imagine how you would start your brand from scratch. What would you build, assuming that money and people weren't factors? Create a roadmap to get there, based on where you are and what you have now. Factor in the speed at which your business moves and this exercise can help you understand what we brought up earlier—whether you need a paintbrush or bulldozer.

And finally, listen. Always listen. Have mechanisms in place that encourage customers and employees to give you honest feedback at any time. And remember to thank them for it even if you don't agree— and especially if it's painful.

CHAPTER 7: DO YOU CARE?

We've spent a lot of time discussing how to create the conditions in which all those most important to your success can care about your brand. Well, almost all of them. What about you?

"Of course, I care," you're thinking. "I bought your book, didn't I?" Or perhaps your first response is, "I started this business, why wouldn't I care?"

Both are valid reactions, but it's important to broach the subject at least. In our culture, so many of us fall into the trap of doing something either because it's expected of us, it's a known entity, or nothing else has presented itself. All too common, too, is the "I'll just do this for a few years…what? It's time to retire?" syndrome.

What I'm saying is that a bit of pragmatism is needed when we make important decisions. As you may have noticed, I am not an Oscar-winning actor, which was certainly the expectation my 10-year-old self had. Nor did I become the next Tom Brokaw, as my grandmother predicted. Just because we are not following our childhood dreams doesn't mean that we have sold out. We just got honest with ourselves.

Nonetheless, we have to care about what we do. It's a balance, living somewhere between not caring enough and caring too much. But this delicate equilibrium is one that we can achieve. It starts with three personal attributes: authenticity, perspective, and reflection.

Authenticity

We have all seen the facades:

- The pop star who professes her undying love for each and every one of us.
- The politician who feigns a devotion to Jesus when none of his actions suggest he is really as devout as he would like us to believe.
- The checkout clerk who says, "Have a nice day" so mechanically, without making eye contact, that it might as well be a recording.

Insincerity is alive and well in our society, so much so that we often do not bother to ascertain the legitimacy of people's words and deeds. Looking beyond the context of marketing and branding to our broader existence, we must ask, "When did we lose our ability to connect with one another on real, meaningful levels?"

As Abraham Lincoln said: "You can fool all the people some of the time, and some of the people all the time, but you cannot fool all the people all the time."

Even if you're working 16 hours a day, reinvesting all your cash into your business and giving it all your focus, it won't last if you do not, at your core, care passionately about what you're doing.

People see right through insincerity. None of the actions we've spoken about in this book will stick if they're not rooted in your authenticity.

Why does sincerity matter? It matters because the type of caring we've outlined in this book is dependent on the genuine sincerity to form, thrive and sustain itself.

The case for sincerity is pretty straightforward, as we can observe by looking at why it matters when creating and growing brands and businesses—as well as in life itself.

Stand out

How do marketers get attention for their brands? They stand out. They continually find new messages, along with new ways and places to deliver them. All marketers must stand out. To brazenly paraphrase marketing guru Seth Godin: You drive down a road and see a cow, you barely notice it. You see a purple cow and you stop.[41]

In a world where insincerity and cynicism reign, what would stand out more than genuine caring? Look at Domino's Pizza and its now-famous declaration that their pizzas tasted bad. Can you imagine the behind-closed-doors discussions that led to that?! For those who don't know the story, here it is. For those who do, feel free to skip the next two paragraphs.

Domino's CEO Patrick Doyle set about improving the company as soon as he arrived at the helm in 2010. One of his first tasks was to address why the company's share price had remained in the doldrums over the previous few years. Interviews with focus groups indicated that Domino's product was almost universally unloved, with the sauce being compared to ketchup and the pizza's dough to cardboard.

Faced with this negative feedback, Doyle made the unprecedented move of apologizing to customers via a series of candid ads in which he said: "Yeah, we suck." For a short time, it was fodder for laughs on late-night chat shows, but Doyle had tapped into something that resonated with his customers more than cheap jokes: sincerity. People actually loved it—a company that raised its hands and, in effect, said, "You're right—and we'll change!" Change they did, and Domino's share price began to rise once again.

Obviously, not everybody should declare themselves fakes and start over. Besides, that specific approach was no longer novel once

Domino's had used it. The key may be to find out how you can use sincerity to stand out and, in the process, earn everyone's care.

Then there's at British Airways CEO Willie Walsh, who refused to take a bonus for two years, admitting simply—and to everyone who saw and heard his commercials—that he didn't think he deserved it.

Karma

If the case for sincerity is not made yet, let's talk about karma. Karma refers to the spiritual principle of cause and effect through which the intentions and actions of an individual (cause) influence the future of that individual (effect). It is believed that good intentions, coupled with good deeds, will eventually produce good karma, resulting in future happiness. Meanwhile, the combination of bad intentions and bad deeds will certainly contribute to bad karma and result in future suffering.

Karma is, as they say, a bitch. You cannot continually send negativity into the world and expect the world to give you back positivity. It just doesn't work that way. Besides, negative energy drains you, while positive energy sustains and supports you. Check it out for yourself.

Perspective

When did so many of us seemingly lose our perspective on what's important in life?

Once upon a time, nearly everyone worked to survive, and obviously that is still the main driver for most people. But how do we define "survival" these days?

Perspective can go a long way. I recently had lunch with a former colleague. She joked that she had become known at her new company for dropping the following bomb, whenever indecision would creep into the analytical process of a meeting: "People, we're not saving lives here. No one is going to die in any of the possible scenarios we're looking at." Perspective.

Once, when working at a multinational corporation, I was sent to an intensive, week-long executive training program—an event I referred to as our "reprogramming." Joking aside, the training was very well done. We met from 8 a.m. to 10 p.m., Sunday through Friday, and covered practically every topic relevant to the up-and-coming executives of the time. Throughout the week, we heard from corporate leaders and academics, everyone an expert in his or her field. One such expert was the renowned business coach, Marshall Goldsmith.

I recall Dr. Goldsmith's advice more clearly than any of the other experts. Despite the fact that our company was paying him, he pushed home this seminal message: Our company is not going to hold our hands on the last day of our lives. The people who will are the ones who deserve our full attention now, not our jobs.

That stuck with me.

Now, I openly admit that I often lose perspective and get caught up in my own monetary goals. I fall victim to comparing myself to others. It's what we do in this culture. However, as long as we work to keep it in check, we'll be fine.

Here are some ways we can achieve that:

- **What's wrong with being Number Two?** Somewhere along the way, our work, our efforts became invalidated if they weren't in the number one spot. Is being number one the only way we can validate our work?

- **How much money is enough?** Howard Schultz of Starbucks made this remarkable statement in a 2016 interview with *CBS This Morning*: "Here's what I believe: we can't be in business just to make money. We must balance profit with conscience and humanity and benevolence and do what's right for our people and our communities. We can do all those things and create long-term value." 25[42]

- **Are we guilty of caring too much?** Remember the startup owner who expected every applicant to see the company as it will be one day and not as it is now? On one hand, this enthusiasm reflected a great attitude, the kind of passion, vision, and commitment needed to make any organization successful. But there was an obvious disconnect between what this man was feeling and expressing subjectively and what I, dispassionately and objectively, observed about his situation.

We must constantly remind ourselves—whether we are involved in a startup or a massive conglomerate—that while we live and breathe our work and our brand, most others do not.

That's why successful brands rely on research by third parties to help them see themselves and their brands the way their clients and prospects do. You would never go to an interview without first looking in the mirror or asking someone how you look, right? What if you had spinach in your teeth? What if you'd cut yourself shaving? Only a mirror or another person could save you from that embarrassment.

Researchers and consultants are the mirrors you should use before you go to your clients and prospects for the kind of interview you have with them every single day as they use or consider your products or services. Don't confuse the future with the present. Understand who you are now. And more importantly, understand how others see you now.

Synonymous-ness

Do you care that perhaps your company's brand and you yourself may have become more or less synonymous in the minds of your clients/customers? That can prove problematic for you and your brand for many reasons.

For example, a few weeks into assuming the (unexpectedly vacant) top job at a major company, the new CEO told my client that the brand messaging had to move away from the core theme of his predecessor as soon as possible. You see, the new leader assumed the brand was a synonym for the previous CEO. That is dangerous. CEOs cannot try to make the brand about them, even if they are the founders.

One's personal brand is always different from organizational brands, although many of the elements may appear to be similar. No organizational brand should be seen as the manifestation of a single person, however charismatic or visionary she may be.

There are many reasons for this separation, not least of which is having the ability to survive changes in leadership. Apple survived the loss of Steve Jobs because the brand was more than him.

Reach can also become a challenge. If your brand is trying to connect with a broad range of people, using the attributes of just one person makes the job much harder.

Then there's the matter of market change. For whatever reason, your offering may suddenly begin to appeal to a whole new segment of the population. With a brand strategy tightly defined around a person, you might have to start from scratch. With a broader, more encompassing one, you will have more time to tweak your messaging gracefully, not change it outright.

Finally, and perhaps most importantly, it's always vital to remember that the brand is everyone's responsibility. It doesn't matter whether an employee comes into contact with customers every day or never, everyone at an organization must think of it as theirs. When companies build the brand around the character or charisma of one person, it's a lot harder to rally the troops.

"I have looked in the mirror every morning and asked myself: "If today were the last day of my life, would I want to do what I am about to do today?" And whenever the answer has been "No" for too many days in a row, I know I need to change something."
— Steve Jobs

Looking inward

Let's talk about you now. You the person, not the marketer. What are you doing? On this planet. In the moment.

For most of us, making a living is a requirement of, well, living. We need to work to provide for our families. But is that all you want? To make a living?

Who says there's only one dream job out there for each of us. Perhaps there are many? Personally, there are plenty of options out there for me that would pay my bills and could keep a smile on my face. Writing this book is one, speaking to people about branding concepts is another.

Why is this important? Why do I have to care to earn caring from others that will build my brand and my business?

Looking outward

The idea of rethinking the problems we solve is nicely summed up by the wise Dr. Seuss:

"Unless someone like you cares a whole awful lot, nothing is going to get better. It's not."

I constantly talk to new entrepreneurs who are creating businesses that generate profits while also serving the common good. One was creating a connection between individuals, corporations, and nonprofits around a form of personal wellness. Her idea was unique, viable and had the potential to make both a profit and transform individual lives and careers.

So, what about you? Can you build a business—a brand—that seeks to solve social problems? Every business should, at some level, devote significant resources to making something that is important to its customers. Every brand should seek to make the customer feel something positive. How much easier, how much more potent would that be if there were a genuine, meaningful way not just to meet the customer's immediate need or solve his or her current problem, but also to bring long-term improvement to something bigger than themselves?

For a long time, we in the for-profit sector have thought about "giving back" to the community in a vacuum, believing that simply writing a check would get that job done. Of course, corporate sponsorships are crucial to the survival of many nonprofit causes, and in no way should that change. But I'm suggesting that we challenge ourselves, to think more broadly about what we do, the problems we solve, and how, as Dr. Seuss would say, we can combine that to "care a whole awful lot."

Care packaging

The entire premise of this book comes from my belief that for a brand to sustain itself in healthy ways and to grow, everyone associated with the brand should care about what it stands for, how it presents itself to its marketplaces and what makes it unique.

But if we step back to consider that hypothesis, what jumps out as an obvious common theme? For me, it is this: Why on earth would we want to waste our precious time and energy doing something don't care about? If we pour passion and pride into our work, if we forego easier and perhaps more lucrative paths to do what we love, shouldn't we do so in a way that naturally fosters an attitude of caring from those most important to our success?

In the end, the key to earning people's care is really about showing respect everywhere and valuing the time and contributions of everyone, including ourselves.

ABOUT THE AUTHOR

Douglas Spencer has spent more than 20 years working with professionals from around the world in many verticals such as financial and professional services, SaaS, high tech, education and healthcare. His brand strategy consulting business, Spencer Brenneman, helps brands in transition—whether creating a new brand from scratch, retooling an existing one or bringing two established brands together. Before starting Spencer Brenneman, he was Vice President, Global Head of Brand Management for Thomson Reuters. Douglas is a frequent speaker on how strong brands improve business performance through strategic alignment, employee engagement, brand governance, verbal and visual identities, and more. He lives in Boston.

END NOTES

[1] Freud, S. (1915), translated by Strachey, J. (2005). On Transience. Freud's Requiem. www.freuds-requiem.com

[2] Salter Ainsworth, M. D. & Bell, S. M. (1970) Attachment, Exploration, and Separation: Illustrated by the Behavior of One-Year-Olds in a Strange Situation. Journal of Child Development, Vol. 41 (1)

[3] Langner, T., Schmidt, J.,; Fischer, A. (2015) Is It Really Love? A Comparative Investigation of the Emotional Nature of Brand and Interpersonal Love. Psychology & Marketing, Vol 32 (6), pgs 624-634.

[4] Bergland, C. (2013) The Neuroscience of Empathy. *Psychology Today*.

[5] Horowitz, S., and Levinson, J., *Social Principles to Heal the World*, Morgan James Publishing (April 19, 2016)

[6] Fink, L., "Annual Letter to CEOs," www.blackrock.com/corporate/investor-relations/larry-fink-ceo-letter, accessed April 2018

[7] Garrad, L., Chamorro-Premuzic, T, "How to Make Work More Meaningful for Your Team," *Harvard Business Review*.

[8] "Apprehensive millennials: seeking stability and opportunities in an uncertain world," The 2017 Deloitte Millennial Survey, copyright 2017

[9] Porath, C., Perason, C., "The Price of Incivility" *Harvard Business Review*, January/February 2013 issue

[10] Dabitch, "Mother NY puts their mothers on billboards for Mothers Day" May 2, 2016, adland.tv/ooh/mother-ny-puts-their-mothers-billboards-mothers-day, accessed, April 2018

[11] "Build a better, more productive workplace with an employee engagement survey," www.surveymonkey.com/mp/employee-engagement-survey/, accessed, April 2018

[12] Mehta, D., Mehta, N., "Employee Engagement: A Literature Review," Economia. Seria Management Volume 16, Issue 2, 2013

[13] Kumar, J.A. (2012). Employee Engagement, Saaransh, RKG Journal of Management, 3(2).

[14] Kim, R. "How Important is Building a Community at Work?," Copyright © 2016 Gusto

[15] Conboy, K., Kelly, C., "What Evidence is There that Mentoring Works to Retain and Promote Employees, Especially Diverse Employees, Within a Single Company?" Cornell University IRL School, Fall 2016.

[16] Journal of Vocational Behavior, Volume 83, Issue 1, August 2013, Pages 106-116

[17] Mohan, B., Norton, M., Deshpandé, R., "Paying Up for Fair Pay: Consumers Prefer Firms with Lower CEO-to- Worker Pay Ratios, Harvard Business School, Working Paper 15-091

[18] "Advertising to the over 50s - how should we do it?" www.gransnet.com/online-surveys-product-tests/advertising-to-over-50s-survey, accessed April, 2018

[19] Spencer, D., "The B2B Brand Strategy: B2B businesses are giving their brand strategies serious focus" January, 2017.

[20] "LinkedIn introduces Career Advice feature," news.linkedin.com/2017/11/linkedin-introduces-career-advice-feature, November 15, 2017, accessed April 2018

[21] Meister, J., "How Deloitte Made Learning a Game," Harvard Business Review, January 02, 2013.

[22] Ibid.

[23] Buss, D., "Weathering the Storm: 5 Questions with Ford VP Mark LaNeve," http://www.brandchannel.com/2017/09/08/a-family-company-5-questions-with-ford-vp-mark-laneve-on-responding-to-harvey/, September 8, 2017, accessed April 2018

[24] Hobbs, T., "Oath's CMO on how it plans to avoid a 'dysfunctional marriage' post-merger," Marketing Week, October 4, 2017.

[25] Aaron, C. (2014). "Comcast goes to Washington...and flops." The Huffington Post, October 4, 2014.

[26] McKinsey (2013). "Organizing the Government Affairs Function for Impact." The McKinsey Quarterly, November 2013

[27] Burgess, W. (2016). "A bad reputation costs a company at least 10% more per hire." The Harvard Business Review, March 29, 2016

[28] Ibid

[29] McAllister, C., Uncommon Sense: Are Companies Truly Committed to Social Responsibility?," Nielsen, Perspectives, January 6, 2016.

[30] Ibid.

[31] Spencer, D., "The B2B Brand Strategy: B2B businesses are giving their brand strategies serious focus" January, 2017.

[32] "Examine how and why McDonald's recently decided to rebrand itself in the UK," The WritePass Journal, August 30, 2016

[33] Dan, A., "Inspired Ideas: Xerox Rebranding A Venerable B2B Brand," Forbes.com, July 5, 2011

[34] Dua, T., "Inside Xerox's biggest-ever rebrand," DigiDay, August 28, 2015

[35] Zmuda, N., "Ad Campaigns are finally reflecting diversity in the U.S.," Advertising Age, March 10, 2014.

[36] Goyette, B., "Cheerios Commercial Featuring Mixed Race Family Gets Racist Backlash," Huffington Post, May 31, 2013.

[37] Jefferson, C., "Cheerios Ad Starring Interracial Family Predictably Summons Bigot Wave," gawker.com, May 20, 2015.

[38] Fortune Editors, "These Are the Women CEOs Leading Fortune 500 Companies," Forbes, June 7, 2017.

[39] Brennan, B., "Top 10 Things Everyone Should Know About Women Consumers," Forbes, January 21, 2015.

[40] Miley, M., Mack, A., "The New Female Consumer, The Rise of the Real Mom," Advertising Age, 2009.

[41] Godin, Seth. Purple Cow: Transform Your Business by Being Remarkable, May 2003

[42] Lee, R., "Starbucks CEO shines light on 'extraordinary' citizens," September 7, 2016, www.cbsnews.com/news/starbucks-ceo-howard-

schultz-upstanders-first-original-series-2016-race-hillary-clinton/,
accessed April 2018